They Called Me Uncivilized

The Memoir of an Everyday Lakota Man
from Wounded Knee

*Walter Littlemoon with
Jane Ridgway*

iUniverse, Inc.
New York Bloomington

They Called Me Uncivilized
The Memoir of an Everyday Lakota Man from Wounded Knee

Copyright © 2009 by Walter Littlemoon

All rights reserved. No part of this book may be used or reproduced by any means, graphic, electronic, or mechanical, including photocopying, recording, taping or by any information storage retrieval system without the written permission of the publisher except in the case of brief quotations embodied in critical articles and reviews.

The views expressed in this work are solely those of the author and do not necessarily reflect the views of the publisher, and the publisher hereby disclaims any responsibility for them.

iUniverse books may be ordered through booksellers or by contacting:

iUniverse
1663 Liberty Drive
Bloomington, IN 47403
www.iuniverse.com
1-800-Authors (1-800-288-4677)

Because of the dynamic nature of the Internet, any Web addresses or links contained in this book may have changed since publication and may no longer be valid. The views expressed in this work are solely those of the author and do not necessarily refl ect the views of the publisher, and the publisher hereby disclaims any responsibility for them.

ISBN: 978-1-4401-6278-7 (pbk)
ISBN: 978-1-4401-6276-3 (cloth)
ISBN: 978-1-4401-6277-0 (ebk)

Printed in the United States of America

iUniverse Rev. 08/26/09

Contents

Foreword vii
Preface xiii
Chapter 1.   To Remember 1
Chapter 2.   Who They Were 11
Chapter 3.   My Father's Drumming 17
Chapter 4.   My Mother's Determination and Generosity 25
Chapter 5.   They Taught Me Indian 31
Chapter 6.   Learning to Be Civilized 37
Chapter 7.   Culture Shock 55
Chapter 8.   Losing Ground 61
Chapter 9.   Our Own Worst Enemy 69
Chapter 10. Remembering the Lessons from the Elders 79

Foreword

Walter Littlemoon, an Oglala Lakota, was raised in the context of multigenerational trauma. He and all his relatives were survivors of repeated trauma they were subjected to through federal "Indian" policies. At the age of five, Walter was taken out of the family web of survival, away from everything that was culturally familiar. He was removed from all the incredibly creative and ingenious ways that his family had survived genocide for generations. He was put into a completely strange experience—a U.S. government boarding school for Indians—in which the trauma was repeated daily, systematically year after year. That trauma would be something akin to the child of Holocaust survivors being shipped off to a concentration camp.

In the boarding school environment, Walter was taught to expect the unexpected. He learned that at any moment he could be punished or abused for a reason that didn't make sense to him. He was isolated, not allowed to speak his native language, he had no means of communication, and he was exposed to arbitrary punishment. Walter learned to live in that state where anything could happen and it wasn't going to be good. There was no sense of consistency, no sense of rationale, no sense of safety, or safe relationships, because everything could turn on a dime. They were the same tactics that are used for mind control in places where captors torture political prisoners—tactics designed to break someone's spirit and to generate obedience, allegiance, and identification with the perpetrator who holds power. It was a complete model of power and domination.

Walter's boarding school experience, which he describes in his memoir, exemplifies Complex Post Traumatic Stress, which involves prolonged abuse, trauma and torture. When you are exposed to trauma repeatedly over the course of your development as a child, your reactions to those traumatic events form who you are, how you understand the world and how you understand relationships. Those components are incorporated into your personality. When you hit another trauma, again its' components are added into your personality. Complex Post Traumatic Stress is different than the more familiar problem known as Post Traumatic Stress Disorder (PTSD). The latter is created through an event, like adult sexual assault, after your personality has already been formed. Complex Post Traumatic Stress results from growing up in an environment where you are exposed to repeated trauma that affects who you are as a person. For example, it's very difficult for people who have had childhood exposure (to abuse, trauma, and torture) to have even a little bit of feeling. Feelings can come up as frightening traumatic states, so people tend to avoid all feeling altogether. Disassociation is part of it. People can have entire aspects of their character cut off, or numb, or split off from the rest of their sense of self. It becomes a way of being in the world, a part of how you've survived, how you've coped and who you are, rather than a symptom that doesn't seem like you.

One of the most sure fire ways to induce Complex Post Traumatic Stress in a person is to force the victim to betray himself. What is unbearable about psychological trauma is that you are helpless over this act of violence that is occurring to you. Of greater impact, than the loss of control and the shame of trauma, is when the perpetrators get you to betray your own sense of moral correctness. Self-betrayal causes a person's spirit to become broken.

The boarding school experiences attempted to get the children to betray their culture, their sense of morality and their relationship with the Creator, with nature, and everything they understood to be human. The children in the boarding schools were led to betray themselves. That's why so many came out broken.

Complex Post Traumatic Stress is a normal response to life-threatening circumstances. It is a response to your life being threatened via interpersonal violence, and it leaves a more intense legacy than does surviving natural disasters like fire or flood. It is composed of an alternation (fluctuation) of intrusive symptoms: flashbacks, hypervigilance, startled response, nightmares, and intrusive recall of the event in the form of smells, bodily sensations and images. Those images can appear as whole and real as if they are being lived in the present, in the here and now. They are also different from images in normal linear memory because they can come up in fragments like little pieces of a puzzle rather than as a cohesive whole.

On one aspect of Complex Post Traumatic Stress the intrusive phenomena, intrusive recall. The other side is the disassociative phenomenon, which is the numbing out, spacing out, losing time, and having feelings of being unreal. These two experiences alternate. You can feel everything in black and white or you can feel nothing. You are disconnected from life. That cycle of intrusive symptoms and numbness is the hallmark of Post Traumatic Stress.

People who have Complex Post Traumatic Stress want to avoid triggers or things that remind them of that situation so they're not plagued with those feelings all over again. Their lives become circumscribed, smaller and smaller, in trying to avoid the trauma, until they actually become defined by the trauma in an attempt to avoid it. Social isolation, and isolation in general, is a big component of Complex Post Traumatic Stress. It's a real paradox.

Healing is based on de-shaming and de-stigmatizing the process that caused trauma in the first place. The Littlemoon's are speaking out and giving words and normalcy to this phenomenon that has been kept underground for so many years. The symptoms are cross-cultural and universal. Something happens to your brain that is not culture bound. Yet, treatments are of necessity based on culture. You can't divorce people from their culture. That's why Walter's work could be very important for healing people other than himself, because Walter is walking in two worlds. He's looking at this concept of Complex Post Traumatic Stress and trying to work with traditional native values to find a way to work with the two together.

When working with people in groups, telling your story can be especially healing because you are finally finding words to communicate an overwhelming life experience, that was a wordless, very psychological experience. All of a sudden, you understand Complex Post Traumatic Stress. It puts words to your experience. It helps you to know that some of the nightmares, some of the hypervigilance, the lack of trust, the feelings of betrayal, the numbness, the disassociation, that felt so crazy in your day-to-day life, are actually normal responses to overwhelming circumstances. At last, you can begin to have a way of understanding what you went through and repairing the narrative of your life.

Having a way of talking about something and conceptualizing it, it gives you room to move. You begin to tell your story in a way that makes sense. In telling the story, all the feelings from the past come rushing forward again and physically you relive it. If you tell me the story often, you may go back into the past 100 percent and you may lose the connection between you and me. You actually become all alone with your experience. It becomes disconnected from the currant reality. However, if I see that you're having a very hard time, that you're shaking and not with me, I can say, "Wait a second. Where are you?" You can say, "Hey, I just really got lost. For a minute, I was four years old again." Then we can stop the telling for a minute and reconnect as human beings in the present.

It's complicated, but that will lower your psychological arousal. It will get you out of the flashback and stop you from reliving the trauma. It establishes a type of a relationship and a set of feelings today about what happened to you so that you are not just sucked into the vortex of that traumatic past. It creates a safe context for time and that way you make a conscious choice.

When you make a conscious choice about how you are telling what it was like, you are providing a remedy to that experience of helplessness and you are making an adult choice. In that manner, the experience has shifted and you are not just reliving. To just remember and relive doesn't change the flashback. You need to bring in some sort of adult sensibility.

That's why the Littlemoons are giving so much thought to the importance of the community of Wounded Knee and other Native American communities. When you have a community that can really begin to talk about the effects of the boarding school abuse on the people, you create a healing context. The Littlemoons are looking toward how to create a safe community dialogue so that people are not all isolated in their personal hells. They don't want to create a free-for-all where people are sharing and becoming re-traumatized. They want to do it in a way that helps move toward integration. Walter and his wife, Jane, are working so hard to find concepts of Lakota language that explain

Complex Post Traumatic Stress. For instance, the Lakota word "sica" (meaning "bad") expresses the feeling of out of balance.

Walter, like many Native Americans, has been very isolated for his entire life with the legacy of his experience. He wasn't able to talk about his boarding school abuse. There was no safe context in which to share it without shame and stigma, and he was unable to understand what a profound effect those years of being abducted had on him. Walter writes in his memoir about his time in San Francisco and how empty he felt, how disconnected from things and from life he felt. Not only was the experience being in the city completely bizarre, having grown up on the reservation, but also there was this sense of disconnection and numbness that he and the other natives in the program carried with them. He had numerous flashbacks too. There were certain things that would remind him of what he suffered in the boarding school, and it would all come back. He tried to avoid that.

His suffering, until now, has been alone and in silence. It's only in writing this memoir that he's been able to acknowledge how much suffering he has experienced over the years. There's no way you can survive the destruction of your family, your culture, and your childhood and not be permanently affected no matter how resilient you are.

Jayme Shorin, L.I.C.S.W.,
Associate Clinical Director Victims of Violence
Cambridge Hospital, Harvard Medical School
Expert in psychological trauma.

Preface

They called me Indian, Sioux, savage and uncivilized. I am a human being. I am Lakota. Like thousands of others, my life was turned upside down through the turmoil forced upon me by a U.S. government system designed to destroy my culture. My life has been spent trying to recover, with the help of the Creator and the strength of the moral courage I inherited.

I am an everyday Lakota man. I live in the small community of Wounded Knee, on the Pine Ridge Indian Reservation in South Dakota. I am sharing my life's story to show others how I am healing my mind and heart from the depths of hell created by the years I was forced to attend an indian boarding school where I was repeatedly beaten and tortured.

Over time, I have also come to see more clearly the different forms of abuse suffered by our parents and our grandparents as our original way of life was brought to an end. Abuse over a long time, months to years, to generations is deeply embedded and disturbing and it leads people to suffer a life that is not positive. I'm sharing this because so many people living on this reservation, and other reservations across the continent still suffer. I want them to know it's possible to be free, to gain contentment, and feel like a human being.

I speak in everyday words for I am not a learned person in the manner of college educators. However, neither are most of the other people here and they are the ones I am reaching out to. I am a somber man so I don't talk in a joking way. However, I do talk from my heart.

All my life I have felt as if I've been walking through a thick dark fog. A counselor who helps victims of violence calls that fog "Complex Post Traumatic Stress" and "Multigenerational Trauma." This memoir began as a small endeavor, to simply record my memories for my children. When I started, recollections came back to me in fragments that skipped all over the years, a little here and a little there. I would speak out loud in the privacy of our living room and my wife, Jane, would write everything down. Not far along in the process, I hit an overwhelming block filled with aching, wrenching sorrow. Repeatedly, I'd start with the words: "When I was five years old…" but I couldn't continue. My doctor at the VA told me to keep talking and to let my feelings out. Slowly, over a period of five years, I was able to remember and share more and more of my life. Once the painful memories were revealed, healthier ones surfaced. We cut up the pages that it was written on and pieced my life together. Then the healing began and it continues today.

Now I stand naked before you all. This is my sweatlodge. This is my vision seeking. This is my Sundance. Remember, restore, reach out.

CHAPTER ONE

To Remember

Early one morning, while sitting at the kitchen table greeting a new day, I gazed upward to where the sky becomes deep blue and watched as a solitary hawk scanned the rolling landscape in search of food, his tail feathers flashing crimson in the sun. A patchwork quilt of colors spread out below him, golden fields, dark green slashes of pine, purple, pink, yellow, blue and red wildflowers sprinkled throughout. The hawk circled slowly, drifting downward and lit upon the immense cottonwood tree that stands just outside the kitchen, next to a small meandering creek, we call Mouse Creek. On the distant horizon rose the dark purple cone of Harney Peak where the Heyoka, Black Elk, sat and saw this future time of our people. Closer, less than two miles away, is the mass grave, the site of the last massacre, the one that took place in December 1890; it is a lonely place, windblown and unkempt.

The tree the hawk rested on is solid. Its girth is wider than three men can reach around. It towers into the sky and provides safe haven, comfort, and shelter to many smaller birds and animals. It has been standing here for over one hundred years. That morning, the Tree began again to speak to me in the old way known to the Lakota. Its words came through as strong, heartfelt feelings as if it were saying:

All things that ever happened in this place, Mouse Creek of Wounded Knee, are a part of today. They are not just history, over and done with, as some now think. I stood here listening to the Hotchkiss guns firing farther down the creek, hearing the screams of the people during what is now called the Wounded Knee massacre. I was already a tall tree when your Lakota grandparents, Little Moon and Rattle Woman, first arrived here to live in the late 1800s. Their parents: Iron Heart, Her Red Road, Never Missed and Helps also visited here. Your great grandmother, Iron Teeth, and her daughters rested here under my limbs on their way back to the Lame Deer Agency, where the Northern Cheyenne were placed in Montana.

Through the passing of many days and nights, I have watched your relatives' come and go. They've gathered in groups and singly in the peaceful shade of my branches to restore their strength. Many of them still struggle, like you, to maintain their Lakota identity through all the chaos that has come to this place. I have held on to their stories and held on to who they are.

From that moment when the Tree first spoke to me, I have repeatedly sought its counsel. I have struggled nearly all of my life to overcome what I've come to call my "fear of living," to be able to look at my life as an everyday Lakota man, with all of its negative challenges and find a healthy perspective—one, that can bring me peace of mind and contentment in this modern day. It is with help from the Tree and my wife, Jane, that I share my journey with you. I hope these words will bring a clearer understanding to those of you who have been suffering as I have, that it will educate younger generations, instill a sense of pride in them and strengthen their self-esteem through awakening in them the moral courage of our Lakota elders. I have come to recognize this moral courage lies within us all, waiting to be recognized, waiting to be remembered. It is our elders' legacy to us.

Many people outside of our culture have written books that focus on one aspect or another of Lakota life—our history, our psychology, our spirituality—but something seems to be missing. Few of these books consider who we Lakota really are, what shapes us, where and how we live, and what life is really like for us today.

Originally, we Lakota viewed the world differently from those new to our land. It was a view that gave us a sense of belonging and connection to all things. To the Lakota the earth is sacred and mysterious. All life comes from it. Each part has its own special reason for being, its own power that is considered sacred. Every person, every animal, every blade of grass has a spirit that is positive and can be of help to the others. Our ancestors knew, too, that even the sun, the moon, and all the stars were made the same way, by a great and mysterious power—one that created it all and keeps all things going. They realized this power provided everything they needed and they were grateful to belong to the brotherhood of life here on earth.

Our ancestors depended on each other to share what food they found in order to survive. It wasn't a land of great plenty; it was a land of enough. Because they traveled frequently over the countryside, hunting for meat, gathering the foods that grew naturally, they had few possessions.

In order to maintain harmony and an orderly society our ancestors walked the Red Road, the road to home, the road that faces west toward Heaven, the road of life. Every day of their lives, they lived, talked, thought and acted out the gifts from the Creator. Those gifts included a clear mind and heart from which came keen vision, acute hearing, and thoughtful speech. In order to walk the Red Road they practiced respect for life, strength, determination, persistence, understanding, awareness, and consideration. They cared for each other. They shared with each other. They gave each other privacy and respect. They honored each other. They moved about frequently and so they had little use for material things. Their homes were simple, uncluttered, and practical. They lived in small bands for survival, with simple rules for living peacefully. They gathered in large numbers each year to honor each other, dance, sing, play games, visit and share. In this way, they celebrated life and thanked the Creator.

From birth, children were considered a sacred gift. The whole tribe protected and preserved their safety and welfare. Children were given freedom to roam, play, and discover within the confines of the camp. Everyone watched over them. As they grew, they learned through caring and loving treatment that they had value. They had duties and responsibilities to carry out in order to become contributing adult members of the tribe. It was a wide, all-encompassing brotherhood that they were a part of.

Today I know the Red Road is still the road to home, the road facing west, toward Heaven. However, the walk has changed. Today the Creator's gifts have been clouded and all but forgotten by clutter, waste, dishonesty, disrespect, irresponsibility, lying, backstabbing, finger pointing, killing, and stealing. Through the excuse of drugs and alcohol, children, parents, and grandparents are abused and our spiritual practices are distorted. Now we make others and ourselves unhappy and miserable. We gather to dance for money and to show off. We practice greed. We are letting go of our self-respect, respect for each other, even our respect for life, looking for ways to shorten it and to destroy it. It seems we have forgotten the greatest gift from the Creator—freedom of choice—and have become our own worst enemy.

Again, I sat gazing at the Tree pondering these troublesome thoughts. Once more, I heard, "all things that ever happened are a part of today." This time the Tree added one word:
Remember.

After the Tree spoke, I sat for a long time as the word "remember" played over and over in my mind. The memories I had of my life were fragmented, coming back to me a little bit here and another bit there. It was hard to pull those pieces together to find a beginning point. Yet, as I looked at the tree, I felt as if some understanding within me was waking up.

I remembered my nephew, Tony, had given me a copy of an interview a doctor named Thomas Marquis had done with my great grandmother and I turned to that for direction.

Her name was Iron Teeth. She died in 1928, fourteen years before I was born. She told her story to Dr. Marquis, in October of 1926 when she was ninety-two years old.

When I first read her words, I felt like I was looking at a stranger, although I was impressed by her age. It was hard to comprehend that anyone in my family would be written about in a book, let alone that the woman interviewed by Marquis was my mother's grandmother and that her life had influenced mine in any way. I read the interview with Iron Teeth over and over again. Until I came across her interview, most of my family's history had been lost and I knew I wasn't the only one who felt disconnected from it. Slowly, I began to realize how far removed our family had become from facing the facts and understanding the reality of our history.

My mother had told us a little about her mother's family. I remember Mom visiting with a Northern Cheyenne woman and speaking to her in their language. She had told me that her mother, Mary Iron Teeth, was Cheyenne and that Mary had taken the last name of Iron Teeth in honor of her own mother.

In the beginning of her story, Iron Teeth described a carefree childhood of playing with homemade toys and of gathering wild sweet potatoes, tipsila (turnips) and other root plants for food with her mother. She told of riding horses and traveling far and wide with her tribe as they hunted buffalo and other game animals. But, it was the events in the middle of her life, which caught my attention and stayed with me.

Iron Teeth had married Machoe when she was twenty-one years old and all together they had five children, two sons and three daughters. My grandmother, whose birth name was Laying Medicine, was the last to be born.

For most of their lives, the family members lived within Dull Knife's band of Cheyenne. Iron Teeth told of the band trading in far away places and meeting white people at trading posts. She told of having skirmishes with other tribes from time to time and of the growing advance of the U.S. army into the Cheyenne territory.

When the 1868 treaty was signed, the Cheyenne agreed to a permanent home in the Black Hills. They were promised that all white people would be kept away from them. Yet, the discovery of gold changed all of that and fighting began in earnest for their territory. Over the next few years, following the treaty signing, Iron Teeth told of how she and Machoe left Dull Knife to live at the White River Agency away from the turmoil, but after learning of the victory at the Battle of the Little Bighorn they felt it was safe to return to the Powder River area and join up with Dull Knife again.

Iron Teeth said that the men in the band didn't want to fight. They just wanted to be left alone to care for their families. They thought nobody would bother them in such a far away place.

They were wrong. At that campsite, on November 25, 1876, a general, by the name of Mackenzie, suddenly attacked their village. Just in time Iron Teeth fled up onto a hilltop with her children and stood watching with them as the soldiers gunned down the men, women and children who hadn't been able to escape. As they watched, Iron Teeth and her children saw Machoe shot and killed as he tried to lead his horse out of the middle of the slaughter. In a short time, their village was burned to the ground and nothing was left except smoldering ashes.

The small group of survivors fled into the night and traveled on foot through deep mountain snow for eleven days. Iron Teeth said they had few blankets and a very small amount of dried food, which they divided among themselves. They gutted ponies, and stuffed babies and small children inside them in an attempt to keep them warm. Several froze to death along the way. Finally, the group reached the camp of Crazy Horse who took them in.

The winter was hard for everyone at that camp and when spring came the Cheyenne surrendered. Iron Teeth rarely commented or complained in her story. She seemed to just tell it straight; but at that point, she added how afraid she was of all white men soldiers for they represented the most extreme cruelty.

After the surrender, the Cheyenne were told that they were being sent to live on a reservation fifteen hundred miles to the south, in Oklahoma. Iron Teeth and the others didn't want to go but they had no choice.

The trip took them over two months to complete as they traveled by horse and on foot. When they got to the Cheyenne-Arapaho Agency in Indian Territory (as Oklahoma was called) Iron Teeth said all of them got sick with malaria. They were there from August of 1877 until September 1878. Food supplies were always low. She said that when their men were discovered sneaking out with bows and arrows to get meat, the whole tribe would be punished by having less food given to them. Many of the tribe's members died that year from starvation and malaria.

In September of 1878, Dull Knife and Little Wolf told the agent they were leaving to go home. The agent replied that anyone trying to leave would be killed. The Cheyenne fled anyway. Iron Teeth's sons joined the fleeing band and she and her three daughters went with them. She carried her youngest daughter, my grandmother Laying Medicine, strapped to her back. The child was then three years old.

Iron Teeth counted seven battles with soldiers along the way. More and more of her people were killed, among them more than sixty children. Toward the end of their escape, the band split into two groups. Her youngest son and oldest daughter went with the group that thought it would be best to go to the old Red Cloud Agency, but Iron Teeth and her three remaining children stayed with Dull Knife who felt they should surrender at Fort Robinson. It turned out to be a horrifying mistake.

Once they surrendered, they were told they had to go back to Oklahoma. When they refused, they (149 men, women, and children) were imprisoned in a small log cabin. Repeatedly the "soldier chief" asked if they were willing to go back. Iron Teeth said, "Nobody answered them. The quantity of food given to us became less and less every day, until they gave us none at all. Then they quit bringing water to us. Eleven days we had no food except the few mouthfuls of dry meat some of the women had kept in their packs. Three days we had no water."[1]

On January 10, 1879, realizing that death could result from any choice they made, the group decided to break out of the prison and hoped that some would be able to survive. They were able to breakout once the soldiers were asleep. Snow was on the ground and the temperature was below freezing. Iron Teeth and her middle daughter fled in one direction and her son fled in another, carrying his three-year-old sister, Laying Medicine, on his back. His name was Gathering His Medicine. He was twenty-one years old and her eldest child.

Iron Teeth and her daughter hid in a cave for eleven days before they were captured again. She searched among the people for her other two children. Finally, the three-year old Laying

---

[1] Thomas B. Marquis, *The Cheyennes of Montana*, (Algonac, Michigan: Reference Publications, Inc., 1978), 76.

Medicine was brought in, without her brother. Gathering His Medicine had saved his sister's life by hiding her under dirt and leaves, but the soldiers had found him and shot him dead. When it was over about half of the original group had died.

Twelve more years passed before Iron Teeth and the other Cheyenne were allowed to return to their homeland near the Tongue River in Montana. During that time, they were kept at White Clay Creek here on the Pine Ridge Reservation. Iron Teeth lived out her life in poverty, often short of food. The words she spoke at the end of her interview had a strong impact on me for she had such a dignified way of retelling her life even though she had lived through many terrible changes. She said: "I used to cry every time anything reminded me of the killing of my husband and my son. But I now have become old enough to talk quietly of them. I used to hate all white people, especially their soldiers. But my heart now has become changed to softer feelings."[2]

As I read Iron Teeth's words, I began to remember more of my own life. Memories that I thought I had buried started to rise to the surface of my mind. Slowly I realized my future was limited unless I too could look at my life in a more understandable way. Her words gave me the courage and determination to proceed with my story and to uncover what had caused me to become disrespectful, confused, and fearful. Step by step, as I uncovered the stories of each generation and added them to the memories from my life I began to realize that the trauma we Lakota have experienced for so many generations is a part of who we are today. The confusion and negative impact it has had on us will be there tomorrow surrounding us like a thick dark fog—if we don't start remembering.

---

[2] Thomas B. Marquis, *The Cheyennes of Montana* (Algonac, Michigan: Reference Publications, In., 1978), 81.

CHAPTER TWO

Who They Were

My grandmother, Mary Iron Teeth, was the little daughter Iron Teeth had named Laying Medicine. She was born in 1875, during that time of violence and terror for our people. Mary was sixteen years old before her band of Cheyenne was allowed to return to Lame Deer, Montana. For the twelve years, following the outbreak from Fort Robinson, she, her mother, and her sister, Tazemeo, waited among the Lakota near White Clay Creek on this Pine Ridge Reservation.

Her remaining brother, White Buffalo Robe (later simply called White Buffalo), had been sent to the first Indian boarding school in Carlisle, Pennsylvania. Boarding schools were created by Henry Pratt, a military career man, whose motto was "Kill the Indian, Save the Man." In agreement with the U.S. government, he designed the school in a strict military discipline fashion. He felt that by removing the children from the influence of their families and their tribes, and forbidding them to speak any native language, they could be shaped into the image of the dominant society. By law, families that refused to send their children would not be given food.

White Buffalo completed his education at Carlisle with the ability to speak both Cheyenne and English fluently. Eventually he returned to White Clay Creek where his mother, Iron Teeth, and his sisters had been waiting. In the early 1890s, after twelve years of captivity here, the Northern Cheyenne were allowed to return to Lame Deer, Montana. At that time, Iron Teeth's family separated and much of our family history became lost. Iron Teeth and one daughter choose to return to Lame Deer; White Buffalo married a Southern Cheyenne woman and moved to Oklahoma, and my grandmother, Mary, chose to stay on the Pine Ridge Reservation here in South Dakota. It has been thrilling for me to research this section of my family's history, for I have discovered White Buffalo's grandchildren, my cousins—Herbert, Rochelle, and Beatrice—still living in Oklahoma. To think, more than one hundred years have passed since this side of my family was divided and yet, we, the great grandchildren of Iron Teeth, have found each other and have shared our history.

On the Pine Ridge Reservation, my grandmother, Mary Iron Teeth, met and married George Harvey. My cousins, Raymond and Walter Martinez, remember our grandfather and some of the family history he shared with them. We all have enjoyed one story in particular, I guess because it demonstrates the moral strength within the old timers. Anyway, Raymond and Walter were fascinated hearing our grandfather tell them of how his father, Charlie Harvey, a white man, came to die. Charlie, who had lived in the mid-1800s, was notorious for "going after" many Indian women, whether they liked him or not. The day came when the Indian men had had enough of his actions. They rose up and went after Charlie. They took him to a tree alongside the

Cheyenne River, north of here, just past the remains of the old bridge. There he was strung, upside down, and shot full of arrows until he was dead.

Our grandfather, George Harvey, was born in 1863 while the Lakota were still living free. His mother, American Horse's sister, raised him within her Tiyospaye (extended family) as is the Lakota way. He was called a "half-breed," since he was half Indian and half white.

By the time George married my grandmother, Mary, survival had become very difficult on the reservation. As captives, our people needed to reach out to each other more than ever before. During their lifetime, laws made by the "Courts of Indian Offenses" outlawed polygamy. However, George Harvey chose to provide for and support two wives in the traditional Indian way. The old traditional way of having multiple wives provided strength for the group. By caring for and sharing with each other, they were able to overcome life-threatening conditions.

So it was that George married a white woman, Maggie Circler, in a manner acceptable under U.S. law and then risked the loss of food rations and imprisonment when he also married Mary Iron Teeth in the traditional Indian way. He developed a cattle ranch in Rocky Ford, on several hundred acres near the edge of the reservation, and together the three adults raised fourteen children. George combined both worlds for his children--as best he could. My mother told me that, as the family grew, he built two sleeping houses one for his seven sons to sleep in and the other for his seven daughters to sleep in.

In April of 1917, the U.S. government created another policy that was so preposterous it's funny to me now. During that period of history, while my mother and her brothers and sisters were still under the care of their father, George Harvey, the government was seeking ways to cut the financial obligations brought on by the treaties with the various tribes. The Indian Commissioner, Cato Sells, declared a policy in which people who were more than one half white blood would be declared competent to carry on their own affairs and free up the government from its financial obligations; whereas, those with one half or more Indian blood were declared incompetent and would still be "wards" of the government. For my grandfather, it meant that seven of his children could carry the last name of Harvey, and were considered competent and white by law, while their seven Indian brothers and sisters were given the last name of Iron Teeth and declared incompetent—even though they were all raised together in the same manner.

I know little of my father's father, even though we all carry his name now. Little Moon, or Wicigala in Lakota, was born in 1851. The only story I ever heard about him was that a large number of people camped here at Mouse Creek in Wounded Knee to attend his funeral. People have said the south hill was dotted with tents, and tipis were scattered in among the pines and over the field. Those who came weren't local for they came in buggies and by horse and wagon. After the funeral, many of them gave away their tents, tipis, and food to the people living in this community. Then they all left. My grandfather must have been a man of some sort of status for so many to have attended.

Grandpa Little Moon's wife, Rattle Woman, Snale in Lakota, took the English name, Bessie Little Moon, in 1900. For generations before them, our people had individual names not family names. Lakota names originally were given to describe an attribute of a person and that name could change as the individual grew. To my knowledge, my grandmother, Rattle Woman, was the first in our family to create a last name. She and my grandfather, Little Moon, named their first children: Star, Wears White Robe, Takes Spotted and, my father, Iron Heart. Later they were given the English names of Katie, Emma, Alice and James, when the law required the change.

My grandparents were the first generation of young adults to live within the boundaries of the reservation. All of them were born during the mid-1800s, years of great upheaval and confusion brought about by a more powerful government intent on the destruction of our reverence for life.

Courage to do hard things, sharing with and caring for each other are some of the qualities that make up the old-time Lakota and Cheyenne. The wisdom and knowledge of their elders guided them. The elders recognized that each individual had unique strengths that contributed to the overall well being of the group. They were people with an oral tradition. Their history was not written down. It was spoken, passed down from generation to generation, just as Iron Teeth demonstrated in her story.

My ancestors' tribes had such a simple code to maintain social harmony, and they followed that code without words or thought because it was as natural as breathing. My grandparents were attached to the land they had lived on. They knew the land provided all they needed to live. The plants, the animals, water, air, and humans were all a part of the brotherhood of life on earth.

CHAPTER THREE

My Father's Drumming

The Thunder Beings came and took my father home when I was ten months old. I wish I had memories of him. My brothers, Moses and Ben, remember the day he left, because they were sitting next to him by the stove.

Our family had been to Porcupine on that July day in 1943 and had stopped to rest in a small building belonging to the Catholic Church at the Massacre site. The foundation slab is still there in the grass near the windmill. A single small cloud appeared in an otherwise blue sky. Suddenly, a bolt of lightning shot down through the chimney, blew open the woodstove door, and struck my father dead. Moses and Ben felt its heat. Water rose up and covered the floor—they don't know how—and it was over.

My father, James Little Moon, was born in January of 1894, twenty-six years after the signing of the Fort Laramie Treaty. He went by the nickname of Joe. The little I know about my father I've learned from listening to other people. I have been told he was Heyoka (English speakers might call him a medicine man). The spirits would have come to him in dreams and guided him to work with the Thunder Beings and they would have helped him to accomplish special things for our people. If a man so chosen turns his back to them and doesn't listen, they will send lightening to take him home. It was not an easy thing to be in those days because the rulings from the U.S. Indian Courts outlawing our spirituality were still in effect. Men were punished severely for practicing the traditional ways. Everyone on this reservation was to be Episcopal as declared through President Grant's 1870 "Peace Policy." Those rulings forced our spiritual practices to "go underground" for over one hundred years.

This property that my house is on was allotted to my father in 1904. It is surrounded by the allotments for his mother, Bessie, and his sisters: Sarah, Katie, Emma and Alice. All together, the parcels total more than a square mile. The U.S. government had created the General Allotment Act of 1887 through which the collectively held tribal lands were divided into individual parcels, some blocks of which were made available to outsiders. To this day, much of our land is still held in trust by the U.S. government and is not freely ours.

My older sister, Pauline, remembers living here in the log cabin our dad built. It had one large open room. The style of living was somewhat like that of previous generations who lived in tipis. The cabin stood right where my house is now.

Pauline tells of waking up in the morning to the sound of our father outside drumming and singing, giving thanks to the Creator for the beginning of another day, and of large groups of people who would attend his sweatlodge down by the plum trees. Actually, sweatlodge is a popular English word, in Lakota we say

Inipi, which loosely translates to "making or giving life." Pauline and others have told me that my father's Inipi was a small dome about four feet high that he made out of tree saplings, covered in canvas. Inside he dug a small round pit where a few red-hot rocks were placed. People came to his Inipi to restore their physical health, refresh their spirits, or to seek answers to hard questions. In the darkness of the Inipi, my father would pour water on the rocks to create a soothing steam and then he would pray and sing. The Inipi, (along with the Hanblecha or vision seeking, and the Wiwaci also called Sundance) was outlawed by the federal courts. My father risked imprisonment by conducting ceremonies in his Inipi.

Vickie, who married my oldest brother Al, has told me of the songs my dad made up and sang at powwows. She and all the other young girls loved to listen to him sing. Others remember the drums he made and gave away so that the heartbeat of our people could be heard.

My brother, Ben, remembers our father's large vegetable garden on the other side of the creek, our mother's smaller one near the house, and the root cellar filled with produce. Hogs, ducks, and chickens were also raised to provide food for the growing family. The creek has filled in a lot over the years, but in those days it ran freely, providing all the water we needed, and it had a great swimming hole near the spring.

Moses talks of the racehorses our dad raised and of the fine saddle he won. Ben adds that his herd of horses was big; some were workhorses, Percherons from Lone Hill's herd, to pull the plow for gardening and the wagons for traveling. Our dad trained them all in the corral he had built down by the great bank at the creek. Everyone had horses in those days and most of them roamed freely, for it was mostly open range. Because of that, they reproduced in the natural way without people choosing and planning as they do today. The people back then didn't worry about anyone stealing their herds because, though there were no brands, every man knew his own horses and there was respect for each other. In those days, nobody fought over horses. One year a huge, coal-black stallion that no one recognized wandered onto our property. He gave our dad a lot of fine young horses.

My father often told my brothers and sisters stories that had been passed down to him from his father. The most memorable was about his grandfather and the coyotes. Dad's grandfather had been out with a hunting party when they were attacked. He was shot in the upper leg and fell unconscious from his horse. The others left him for dead. After a long time of lying there, he came to and saw two coyotes sniffing the other bodies. When they approached him, he lay still too weak from lost blood to move. He must have passed out again for the next thing he knew the coyotes had taken hold of the back of his shirt and were dragging him off. They came to a hole on the side of a bank, which was their den, and pulled him in.

About eighteen months later, when he finally returned home, he told of how those coyotes licked his wound to clean it, brought him food, and nursed him back to health. During that time, he learned how to communicate with them. No one knows how that was done. Just before he left the family of coyotes approached him one last time with a message. They told him that, as a reminder of the connection they had formed with him, one child in every generation of his family would have the eyes of a coyote.

As long as Dad's grandfather lived, he kept in touch with the coyotes. He would meet with them on a distant hill, and they would still approach him to tell him if storms were coming and in times of hardship, they'd tell him where the game was more plentiful. In return, they asked him to share some of the meat with them and to leave it on a certain hill, for they were suffering too. His ability to communicate with them helped his band of Lakota to survive in hard times. To this day, our family has seen one child born in each generation with the eyes of a coyote.

While I was growing up, people in the community would also tell me stories of my father. They'd often remark, "Your father would always go the extra mile to help a person." Many of them liked to tell me of the night he found an old man named Yellow Shield lying out near Fast Horse Creek. They'd always start with the words: "Your dad sure had a good sense of hearing." One night, he was out visiting a friend about a mile east of his home, near where the mountain lion has been roaming in the pines. It was around Thanksgiving. Frost lay on the ground, and the temperature was dropping below freezing. Just as he and his brother-in-law, Red Bear, mounted their horses to go home, my father thought he heard a faint sound. He strained to listen and, sure enough, he heard a man calling from a distance. He and Red Bear, he rode over the pasture, stopping a number of times so he could listen in order to maintain direction. After traveling a couple of miles, he finally located seventy-year-old Yellow Shield lying on the bank of a ravine near Fast Horse Creek. He had fallen from his horse and broken his hip. My father stayed with him while Red Bear rode off to find someone with a car to help transport the old guy to the hospital. It was amazing that he was found and survived. He had been lying just over three miles from where my dad had first heard his call.

Howard Wounded Horse, one of the older residents of Wounded Knee, always called my father "Uncle Joe." Howard was a long-distance runner in his younger days. There were races on the reservation then, and people liked to place bets on the runners. When Howard was going to run his first race, they considered him the underdog and no one would bet on him. He said "Uncle Joe" bet one horse on him and told him he would win. As Howard described it, he felt a burst of energy in his body when he heard those words. As the race began, he was last, but he thought of my dad's words and his body felt lighter and faster. Before long, he was passing the others, and, to his amazement, he won the race. Howard told me that, because my father believed in him, he was able to do it. In races after that, he became an even better runner. As long as he lived, he always remembered the faith my father had in him.

The Pine Ridge Reservation was created under federal status; state law enforcement has never been allowed to cross over its boundaries. Like a magnet, it has attracted outlaws on the run looking for a place to hide. One outlaw, a known cattle rustler, chose Wounded Knee to live in. He was allowed to pass through our property on the condition that he close the gate to the pasture so the horses wouldn't get out. I don't know how many times he was told to close that gate, but each time he came through, he'd brazenly leave it open. Finally, Dad waited for him one day, watching from off to the side. Sure enough, again he left the gate open once he had passed through. This time, my father was ready. Stepping forward, lasso in hand, he roped the guy, pulled him off his horse, and whipped him with the rope. It happened again and again after that, and each time the rustler ignored the request to close the gate and dealt the same medicine. Finally, my oldest brother, Al, took a battery and some wires and somehow rigged the gate. When the rustler put his hand on the gate the next time he passed through, the charge knocked him down. After that, he always closed it behind him.

In the 1930s, during the Depression, John Dillinger showed up at our door with another man and a woman. He wondered if my father had a place they could stay for awhile for they were tired and needed a rest. I've been told that my father considered Dillinger to be a man like the English Robin Hood, who robbed from the rich to help the poor. Pauline remembers that the root cellar was rearranged and bedding was put in for them. It was something our parents did for many others who came needing a place to rest, though this time a pile of trash was added in front of the doorway to disguise it. The two Yellow Hair brothers came over, took Dillinger's car down among the chokecherry trees and covered it with branches. Pauline also remembers airplanes flying around overhead. After awhile the food supply was running low and Dillinger gave my father some money to buy more groceries. The storekeeper, at the little store in Denby, seven miles south of Wounded Knee, became suspicious when he was handed a fifty-dollar bill as payment for no Indian ever had that kind of money. He asked where the money had come from, but my father kept his mouth shut. The storekeeper called the nearest bank, which was in Gordon, Nebraska, to verify the serial number on the bill. When my dad returned home, he mentioned this to Dillinger, and soon after that all three people packed up and left. Rumor has it that they stopped in Porcupine to fill their gas tank and proceeded east from there.

These are the few stories I've heard about my father. I look at his picture wondering what he was like. I see Moses's eyes looking back at me, but I also see my nose and mouth. I know we got our height from him too, because they've told me he was a tall man. I think of him as a man who provided well for his family, who cared about people and was generous. I see a courageous man who stood up for what he believed in, for he practiced Lakota spirituality as a whole way of life even risking imprisonment by using the Inipi, for it was outlawed in those days by the U.S. government. Why did the Thunder Beings take my dad home? What more was he to do?

CHAPTER FOUR

My Mother's Determination and Generosity

Life must have become very hard for my mother after my father's death, but I wasn't aware. Self-pity wasn't in her nature. She gave me the impression that this was how life was for all people and I was content. Her name was Rosa. She was born in 1902, as one of Mary Iron Teeth's seven children; Mom was the granddaughter of Iron Teeth. For years, I admired her more than any woman I knew.

She was a tiny woman, just shy of five feet, yet she had a presence of such dignity and determination—she could fill a room. No matter what tasks she worked on, she kept her appearance neat and tidy, wearing clean flower-print dresses, and a crisp blue checkered apron, topped by colorful sweaters of blue, orange, or plum. Even on hot days, she'd wear nylon stockings and sturdy black shoes, with her hair rolled up into a bun held in place with blue-beaded hair combs. I remember watching her take the combs out of her hair at night. It would release from their hold and fall over her shoulders, down her back, in thick black waves. I felt so peaceful in those moments, when I'd watch Mom brush her hair.

I was the youngest of my mother's ten children. Three had died before I was born, Raymond, Susie, and Grace. By the time I was three all the rest were away from home. My oldest brother, Al, was full-grown and the others, Pauline, Wilson, Francis, Moses, and Ben, were at the Oglala Community High School (OCHS), the U.S. government boarding school, in the village of Pine Ridge. Mom also raised Teresa, my father's daughter from his first marriage to Lucy Catches. Teresa was quite a bit older than the rest of us, yet she always called my mother "Mom" and frequently came back to visit her.

My mother was a hardworking woman and did what was necessary to provide for her family. One year she and I traveled to Mirage Flats, Nebraska, where we lived in a tent while she picked potatoes for a farmer. Winter came early that year. The snow fell, and we weren't able to return home until the spring. We spent the winter living in that tent and somehow she was able to keep us warm and fed.

I remember days when the sky would suddenly flash and then a loud boom would fill the air. Mom would quietly say, "They're bombing again," and put her hand on my shoulder to reassure me. As I grew older, I asked her what that noise had been. She told me that the army had used some property during the war to practice bombing. Some of that land had belonged to her and her brothers and sisters, but the U.S. government had bought it from them—for pennies an acre. When her brother, my Uncle Ben, would visit, he often reminisced about his love for that place and longed to buy it back. However, he never was able to for it had become a dangerous place, littered with unexploded bombs.

Just before I went to school in 1947, my mother married again to Louis Good Medicine. We moved from our log home at Mouse Creek down the hill to his two-room WPA house by Wounded Knee Creek, near the massacre site. He died four years later. I don't remember much about him.

Louis had five daughters who became my stepsisters, but they were all much older than me and mostly gone from home. To make ends meet Louis sold all of my father's horses. Until then, we had traveled everywhere by horse and wagon. Going for supplies in Gordon, Nebraska, thirty miles away, was a two-day trip. We'd stop to camp overnight at a place called Midway, as many others did at that time.

Everything to maintain a home was done by hand in those days. My mother's time was completely filled. When we boys were home from school, we would haul water from the creek every day and gather wood for the fire. During winter months, it could be really hard to find enough wood. We couldn't be fussy. My mother would hang a blanket over the doorway connecting the two rooms. We'd live in just the one room, so as not to have to heat both of them. Even with that, there were a lot of mornings when the water in the bucket had ice on it.

My brothers and I were expected to supply meat to supplement Mom's food supplies. The ammunition we used was precious and hard to come by, so we'd take care in what we shot. It never occurred to us to kill for the pleasure of killing or to shoot an animal or bird as a game or for a trophy. Through that strong need, we became observant and careful, even when we weren't hunting.

Mom washed our clothes by hand and hung them outside on a line to dry. She used a treadle sewing machine to make quilts with material she salvaged from our worn out clothes. I remember helping her as a quilt neared completion. She and I would move the furniture back to the edges of the room and spread out the cloth on the floor. She'd give me a long needle threaded with darning yarn and have me tie knots in a pattern to join the layers. Then she'd finish the quilt by hand-stitching the edges closed.

Our mother always had a large vegetable garden. Every morning she'd send us out with a bucket to fill in the creek and we'd cast water on the plants with a ladle. Our days would get really busy when the vegetables began to ripen for then Mom would start canning them to store in the root cellar for the winter. We always had to make sure she had enough wood and water on hand to cook and pack the produce in sterilized jars. It seemed there was always enough food to share with anyone who came around, especially other boys from the community who had growing appetites. Even at the end of a winter, when our supplies were low, she would share our food and give people a place to stay, for my mother's home was a gathering place.

Mom loved planting flowers. Vines of morning glories grew up one side of the porch for shade and she planted bright-colored flowers in a star-shaped bed. She hung curtains in her windows and, because no one else did, people teased her, in a gentle way, saying it came from her white grandfather's blood.

Our mother taught us to watch where and how we put our feet as we walked through the woods and fields, to take care to bend branches and not to break them, to watch out for certain plants and not trample them, to be on the alert for rattlesnakes and walk around them. Even her flower garden had paths for us to walk through or to sit among the flowers, for she knew that children would be drawn to their beauty but had to learn how to enjoy it and not to destroy it.

My mother did have a temper and she could be moody. I never gave much thought to it, probably because she never directed her anger at me. She used to say, "Words are like the wind, they come and go." And we'd know someone had annoyed her. I remember one time a man had died and none of his relatives came to the funeral. Some months later, when it was learned that he had left some money, one of the women showed up to claim it. Without hesitating, Mom grabbed the woman by the shoulder, lifting her high on her toes, walked her to the door, and shoved her out. After that, Mom located the man's two surviving sons and saw to it that they received their inheritance. The search for them took her nearly two years.

I don't remember my mother ever hugging me. Yet, she had a way of putting her hand on my shoulder that gave me such peace and comfort. She maintained the Lakota values of caring and sharing through confusing and changing times. She carried herself with dignity, used common sense, was generous, and taught us to "go ahead regardless." All of her sons, except Al who had broken his collarbone, joined the U. S. armed forces, during the Korean and Vietnam wars, because she had instilled in us a duty to the people and the land.

She passed away in 1981, yet she has never been forgotten, and still her name, Rosa, is said in a tone of voice filled with respect by everyone who knew her.

CHAPTER FIVE

They Taught Me Indian

When I was a child, we learned to be Lakota in a natural way, as easy as breathing. No one sat us down to preach at us. Adults guided us as life presented different situations. The older men in the community, Looking Horse, Left-Handed Jimmy, Tall Charlie, and others, would gather at the trading post and, through listening to their casual conversations with each other, we'd learn from them how to watch nature for information about storms coming, seasons changing, and all sorts of things. In that manner, we learned a respect for nature.

Sometime back in the early 1950s, before space shuttles rose into the sky, Left Handed Jimmy told us the most unusual reason to respect nature. He said we are the youngest species of life here. We're different and not capable of keeping ourselves alive, for we came from the red world onto this blue world. All the animals and other forms of life here give to us and sacrifice for us to help us live.

Along with those conversations, the elders would often take the time to tell us humorous stories about animals, mostly about the tricksters, Iktomi the spider, and Miashla the coyote, who were always together, and whose conduct and thinking are often reflected in people. In those stories Iktomi would stubbornly hold on to a negative, dishonorable, twisted lifestyle and he'd try his best to convince others that his way was the most honorable. He'd twist situations around by manipulating people's minds, and in doing so, take away their pride, dignity, honor and individuality. Time and again, Miashla would wait patiently and respectfully for the moment when he could step forward to remind people of the natural, positive way. In that manner he'd help to restore what they were losing—their honor, dignity and pride.

Through those stories we learned about human nature. We learned that positive and negative choices are always available in life. We came to recognize the language of those who would approach us to take advantage of us by lying, cheating, or stealing. Most important, through those stories we were being taught to use laughter to assist a person who was going through a crisis, who was depressed, or who needed to look at life in a healthier way. Our use of humor was always that way. It was never used as a put down or to mock another person.

Sometimes the older men would bring us boys along with them for a day of fishing. I remember Left-Handed Jimmy taking my cousin, Cedric and me up along the Wounded Knee Creek, about a mile from our home. We came to a nice little place just past some trees, where the bank opened up and the grass moved back. He told us to stay quiet so the fish wouldn't be frightened away and we sat down holding our poles steady with the lines in the water. As time passed, a deer strolled up on the bank opposite to us. His tail and ears were flicking back, and forth and clumps of fur hung off his skinny body. He may have been sick or very old, for he wasn't smooth-coated and fleshed out. Yet, as he stood there looking at us, my eyes made contact with his. I saw such beauty and calmness in those dark pools. It gave me a surge of joy. The ground I sat on felt softer, and the sweet, fresh smell of the plants seemed to increase and fill the air. Those moments of gazing into his eyes felt like coming home after a long absence.

We boys often found pleasure in roaming through the woods and fields. I recall one such day for my friend Harold High Pine and me. We were walking through a stand of pines when we heard a lot of pheasants calling up ahead, so we followed the sound. At the edge of the pines, we peered through some branches and down a hill onto a field. There we saw a huge flock gathered in the green and gold summer grass. The pheasants had formed a circle. Those on the outside of it were hopping up and down, flapping their wings and calling out in unusual sounds that seemed to me like they were singing. In the center was a single row of pheasants running counter-clockwise in a perfect circle. As we watched, some would part from that circle and run in a path straight across from the east to the west. Then they'd rejoined the formation. Soon others would proceed to separate out doing the same, only this time run in a line from north to south. All the while those on the outside continued jumping up and down, flapping their wings and calling out.

Harold and I stood for a long time perfectly still with our mouths open in amazement as the show went on and on. Finally, we tired and quietly pulled away. As quickly as we could, we ran to his father, anxious to share our exciting discovery. Mr. High Pine smiled at us and said, "You've seen pheasant dancing." He told us it happens from time to time, not every year, but in those years when their food is plentiful and their numbers have grown large. Then they have no fear and they are happy. They celebrate by gathering to dance and to sing. Mr. High Pine added, " We Lakota do the same."

The following day, Harold and I went back to the spot, hoping to see it again. The pheasants were gone. Yet, in the spot where they had gathered, remained a perfect circle about ten feet in diameter with a plus sign crossing its center remained in the field. The mark of the design was about three inches wide where their feet had worn the grass down to the dirt.

During those summer months, when we weren't at school, homes were open to us, food was shared; Lakota was spoken everywhere. We'd swim in the creek, roam the woods, climb trees and play with toys we'd make from scratch. On occasion, a woman we called Tall Jenny would come walking down the road bringing candy in a pack on her back. We never knew where she lived or where she came from, but it was certain we were glad to see her. We'd help our mother gather the wild fruits as they ripened: plums, buffalo berries and chokecherries. In that gentle atmosphere, we learned through watching the actions of the adults to care for each other, to share with each other, to respect, and to honor life above all else.

From time to time, as I grew, death would come to families, and I would watch the strength of our Lakota faith rise to the surface for all to see. I learned from my mother and other adults that when death comes our spirit goes home to join the ancestors and our body stays on earth to feed other forms of life—a mystery we will all come to know eventually. For centuries, the bodies of our deceased were placed up on scaffolds instead of being buried in the ground. Time has changed our traditional ways though, to meet modern-day circumstances, and now we bury our dead. The last corpse to be placed on a scaffold was that of a woman who died in the 1940s. Her body was put up in the lone pine down the road from here for three days before her family buried her in the ground.

I was taught that when death comes it is a time for us to give away to others. We give away in a respectful manner to honor the deceased, as if to say, "See all these beautiful things? None of them are as meaningful to us as the person we have lost. The Creator provides everything we need to survive and we trust all we need will still be provided once again."

One elderly couple, who had lost their only son, gave away everything they owned. Their neighbors gathered around them as they stood in their yard giving away pots, pans, blankets, furniture, horses—everything, even the clothes they had been wearing. At last, they stood naked before those gathered. Two women stepped forward, covered them with blankets, and took them back into their empty home. The next morning the elderly couple awoke to find horses tied to their fence and other items left by their door.

We were taught that the spirits of our ancestors come to take the deceased home. We, who remain, will not speak the name of the dead for a period of time, up to a year, so that person can follow the ancestors home without turning back toward us and getting lost here on earth. After they are home for a while, they will be able to travel back and forth to watch over us and to help us.

Sometimes life can have some cruel twists and turns. The bright and positive memories of those childhood days have stayed buried within me for nearly sixty years. For all those years, I felt a nameless sense of sorrow and longing as if a thick, dark fog covered my mind and heart. In remembering everything, these memories have broken free from the fog's hold and brought me peace. But first, I had to remember and see clearly how I had been shaped and twisted, mentally and emotionally, by something outside of our culture.

CHAPTER SIX

Learning to Be Civilized

Shortly after my fifth birthday in 1947, a shiny gray car pulled up to our home with two strangers in it. My mother was crying. She told me I had to go with those people in the car. I had no warning, no preparation. Perhaps she thought it was best that way or perhaps she wasn't expecting them. I don't know.

I sat in the backseat of the car with my head down, scared to look around, as the men took me for a long drive. They finally stopped at a strange, foreign place with tall buildings. Other children were gathered there. I was overwhelmed by strange smells, sounds of children talking and crying, all the big, tall buildings, everyone speaking a language I didn't understand. There seemed to be no one for me to turn to, no familiar faces. Then, in the confusion, I saw my sister, Pauline, and I ran to her crying. Gently, she told me not to cry, that Mom would come get me in a month. As we stood there, two stern-looking women marched up to us. Pauline told me I had to go with them. When I hesitated because I felt confused, they pushed me along roughly into one of the buildings and abruptly sat me in a chair. Within minutes, all my hair was cut off; I was stripped naked and scrubbed with harsh yellow soap and a stiff brush until my skin was raw. It stung so. The women spoke a language I didn't understand and slammed my back with an open hand when I questioned them in Lakota.

One woman tossed my clothes from home into a box, and the other threw a different set at me, grayish blue coveralls with a trapdoor in the back, a shirt, a set of underwear and great big, brownish shoes. The pants were heavy denim, baggy around my waist and much too short. The shirt had ragged elbows, and its sleeves didn't reach my wrists. When the women were finished with me, I sat off by myself in a big room lined with benches where several boys were sitting. No one spoke. I was too scared to move and just sat as quietly as I could. Sometimes I'd sneak a peek at the others, but mostly I just sat, waiting to go home.

Time blurred. The women led us all to another room where we were each given sheets and two dark blue or gray blankets with big letters in the center that read: U.S. Then they marched us up a flight of stairs to a large room with two rows of metal beds lining the walls. Older boys were standing in there. The women held sticks in their hands and barked out orders in the strange language. Soon they began whipping some of the other boys. I stared at them, unable to comprehend what I was witnessing. I had never seen an adult beat a child. I kept standing there, not knowing what to do. A big boy grabbed me by my shoulder and pointed to a bed. He didn't speak. When the women left the room, he silently showed me how to arrange the sheets and blankets so that one blanket folded in half, placed over the top of the bed, and tucked in on the sides like a cover.

When all the beds were finished, the big boys marched us off again, down the stairs, outside to yet another large building. We were taken up a flight of cement steps to a room filled with boys and girls sitting at long tables eating. A huge fan hung from the ceiling, its blades turning slowly. I had never seen such an enormous place. Off to one side of the room stood a long counter made of steel and glass. Older girls stood behind it dishing out food to a long line of children. The big boys took us over there. We copied what the others in front of us were doing. We picked up trays and put plates and silverware on them, then pushed them along on a metal railing. The food was green, red, and yellow. It smelled awful.

With those trays in hand, we were led as a group to three long rows of tables way in the back of the room. Along the way, we passed children whispering, and shoving each other. As we sat eating the strange-tasting food, I glanced around the room searching for a familiar face, but I found none. I felt overwhelmed. The big boys stood at the end of our table and, when we were finished eating, they led us to an area where we were to scrape leftover food from our dishes into a barrel and leave our trays at a window. Then they escorted us back to the first building, where once again we sat alone in silence, on the benches lining the ground-floor room.

Time passed. A bell rang. The big boys returned and led us up the stairs to our beds. Numbed by the frightening confusion of the day, we silently crawled under our blankets. The lights overhead went out. The silence of the long, dark night was broken only by sounds of quiet weeping. That was my first day of many years at the U. S. government boarding school in Pine Ridge, Oglala Community High School (OCHS). It was an odd name since children from kindergarten age through grade twelve were taught there.

The room began to lighten with the dawning of the second day. As I lay in my bed I could hear other boys stirring in theirs, but none of us got up. We just lay there, waiting. Suddenly the bell from the night rang out sharply, piercing the silence. My breath caught, and my heart pounded. The same two women stomped into the room, still carrying their sticks, yelling out in harsh voices words I couldn't understand. We all leapt from our beds, desperately trying to figure out what orders they were giving. As they strode down the aisle between the two long rows of beds, they grabbed different boys and beat them with their sticks. Those boys had wet their beds. They hadn't been shown the room to pee in, with the strange, shiny, white things on the wall. The women didn't care. They beat and beat and beat. As a group, we stood watching and came to realize by their gestures what the women expected us to do. And so, it was in fear that we washed, dressed, made our beds, and finally marched off together to eat our breakfast in the place with the counter made of steel and glass.

My brother, Ben, who was nine years old, came up to me there. He glanced around first and then spoke to me very softly in Lakota. As quickly as he could, he told me things to expect and how to act, but it was a blur to me. I didn't ask him anything, not even where he slept. I just listened to the comforting sound of his voice and followed him as he led me to a building he called the "Primary" where I was to be taught things. Ben left me standing next to my teacher in a classroom and disappeared as suddenly as he had come up to me.

The teacher was very tall and scary looking. Her gray hair, piled up on top of her head, looked like a beehive. She took me into a small room where, off to the left, was a sandbox and a lot of toys. But I didn't want to touch any of them; I just wanted to go home. The other side of the room had rows of desks with lots of boys and girls sitting at them. My stomach felt tight. I stood there not knowing what to do, and my head ached from the effort it took to comprehend what the teacher was saying.

My memories of those beginning days, filled with the words from a foreign language, are mostly tied to sights, sounds, and feelings. One afternoon, that day or perhaps the next, we were led to yet another classroom. How clearly that moment comes back to me. As I stood just inside the door, a man wearing a long black dress came up suddenly behind me. He grabbed me by the collar on my shirt and the seat of my pants and threw me into the middle of the floor. I still remember how it felt being in the air, as if time had stopped and held me there. Then it seemed as if the floor flew up at me. I still can feel the searing pain on the side of my face when I came crashing down. In that brief moment as I stood inside the entrance looking around at the room, I had forgotten to pay attention to what was going on around me. The only English words I knew were "yes" and "no," which Ben had taught me. I hadn't sat down quickly enough.

Slowly the days passed. The bell would ring to get us up in the morning and to signal it was time to go back in the building in the evening. Some boys would start crying when they heard it. We learned the two women were called matrons and that our beds were in a dormitory named Lower East.

Punishment came at least two or three times every day in the classroom and even more frequently in the dormitory. Everywhere we went we were required to march two by two holding hands—no talking, no laughing, just marching. We were punished for walking on the wrong sidewalk, punished for stepping off it. We had to walk and not run. We were punished for getting our clothes dirty or our shoes scuffed.

There was one place to play, maybe 25 feet square, with a set of swings, a see-saw, and a merry-go-round; its boundaries were guarded on four corners by big boys. Off to the side by some trees was another small area for baseball. We'd use sticks for a bat and make baseballs out of rolled up rags. The football field and gym were kept for the big boys.

If we spoke out of turn, especially if we spoke Lakota, we were hit with whatever the matrons found handy: a belt, a stick, a book, a shoe, sometimes an open hand or a closed fist. Other times we had to pull our pants and underwear down, "just to make sure" we didn't have any protection stuffed in there. We were to bend over holding our ankles, and they would beat us with a belt doubled over, a strap, or a thick board. We called the board the "ape stick"; it was about eighteen inches long, three-quarters of an inch thick with holes drilled into it. The strap was long and thin like a horse quirt.

Every morning we had oatmeal for breakfast. It always had mealy bugs in it. I remember the butter smelling worse than sour milk. We were ordered to line up, boys on one side and girls on the other, no talking was allowed. No matter how hungry, we couldn't eat too fast, because "pigs eat fast," and others wouldn't be able to enjoy their food. If we did, "eat like a pig," our food was taken away and we were told to leave the room. The utensils had the letters "U.S." stamped on them. They were counted at the end of the meal, and if we didn't return a knife, a fork, or a spoon to the kitchen area we had to go back and find them. If we didn't, we'd be beaten. We learned, when we couldn't find our missing utensils, to steal someone else's.

Some of us were sent every Wednesday afternoon to a priest who taught a Catholic catechism class. We were told our parents belonged to the Catholic Church and therefore we belonged to that church too. I never really understood what that word catechism meant, but because the priest repeatedly stressed that we were savages and sinners on our way to hell, I figured catechism was connected to that place.

Saturday mornings were set aside for cleaning the building and picking up trash and leaves on the lawn. In the afternoon you could go to town if you had money, otherwise you had to stay in the building for the rest of the day. So, we'd pass a nickel from boy to boy. We called it "lending money." Before leaving, we'd be searched and then sign out on a paper. After awhile the matrons and the Boys' Advisor started asking what we bought with the nickel when we came back and have us prove it.

On Sundays, we were required to attend church for at least an hour of standing, kneeling, and keeping quiet. We each had a gray suit to wear with a white shirt and tie. Our church shoes were black, and we were told to polish just the toes. I had no idea what a church was about. I'd ask a lot questions but always received the same answer—"Be quiet." Once I wanted to know, If this was God's house, where was God? The priest never said a word; he merely pointed to a light hanging from a chain attached to the ceiling. It was encased in a long tube of green glass. They gave us food after the service, which was the best part, for that hot dog, cup of coffee, and piece of candy, was the only food we'd get on Sunday, except for bread. We'd sneak out as often as we could to steal apples from the storeroom or vegetables from the garden. We were always hungry.

Twice a month our heads would be shaved. The matrons kept our names in a ledger and marked down B for bugs or C for clean. The big boys would laugh at our bald, gray, skinned heads. We'd feel shame and embarrassment.

We would shower in the dormitory basement twice a week, on Mondays and Thursdays; at home, we had bathed more frequently. Twenty or more boys shared ten showerheads at the same time. We'd come out into a dressing room area naked, wrap towels around ourselves, and then be made to line up for inspection. One or two matrons would stand there and tell us to drop the towels so that they could make sure we were clean all over. We even had to bend over so they could check our private areas. I never got used to them staring at us, touching us. There was no privacy. Even in the bathrooms they'd come in and watch us pee. At night, they'd come in the dormitory rooms and stand watching us change into our pajamas. If we turned our backs on them for privacy, they'd whip us.

Beatings were frequent and rarely made sense. If we got an "A" we were beaten for cheating, if we got an "F" we were beaten for being stupid. So, we learned to stay in the middle. The teachers liked to grab us by the ears, twist them, and pull us off the floor by them. Our fingers would be bent backward. We'd be made to kneel on a pencil holding our arms straight out for a long time until our bodies cried in pain.

I remember getting slapped with an open hand on my face and head. I was backed into a corner, and the slapping went on and on, for at least two or three minutes. My mouth and nose bled, my ears rang, and my face felt hot. I had to blink to get my balance back. There were times when they'd cup both hands and slam them simultaneously together over my ears. It would make a popping sound, my head would feel numb and my ears would ring. I remember being knocked down and pulled up again by the hair on the back of my head. The teachers, the matrons, the Boys' Advisor, they all beat us. These acts were things we had no words for in Lakota.

Three months went by, though it seemed to me to be a long, long time. I learned, like the other children had, to avoid all adults, to turn away when they passed by, and to stand quietly. I had become a silent observer, without joy or laughter. Then came the day that never went away.

My brother, Ben, ran up to me as I stood on the playground. He was filled with excitement: "Walter, Mom came! We can go see her!" I looked at him, but couldn't quite place what he was saying. He grabbed my hand and pulled me along with him. When we reached the edge of the school grounds, I stopped. A woman was walking toward us. She looked familiar, like I knew her. I felt drawn to her—she had a warm smile—but as she got closer, I became frightened. I wanted to both run and stay, so I hid behind my brother. Ben turned to me exclaiming: "Walter, it's Mom! It's Mom!" I kept staring at her, trying to connect with his words. I don't remember what she said or how long she stayed, though I know it was only a very short time before she turned away and slowly got into a car. The driver was backing out when my breath caught: In that instant, I knew her.

Overwhelmed with joy, longing, fear and sorrow, I screamed out "Ena!" and started forward to run after her. A matron grabbed me roughly by the shoulder and pushed me stumbling back to the dormitory and down into the basement.

I don't remember much of anything after that except that I didn't want to eat. I couldn't understand why I had to stay. Why couldn't I go home with her? Over and over, I vowed to myself that I would never forget my mother again, no matter how hard they beat me.

I didn't learn much that first year. All I knew was that I wanted to go home. We were told we had to become civilized. As I understood it, that meant we had to wear shoes, eat using a knife, a fork and a spoon, and speak English.

The school year ended in May, usually around the twenty-fifth. Some years we could go home briefly for Thanksgiving and Christmas, but most often we couldn't. We learned to survive in that harsh place by not looking forward or backward, keeping our focus on each moment as best we could. It was too painful to think of home. Yet, as the end of May approached, we'd fight within ourselves to keep the excitement down. We feared the bus wouldn't come or maybe they'd change their minds.

On the morning of the last day, we'd line up outside waiting, anticipating the arrival of the bus. It seemed to take forever. We'd all be the best children, orderly and quiet, as we stepped aboard. When at last it started toward home, we would turn and grin at each other. Soon the bus would be filled with the happy sounds of children talking and laughing together.

As the bus rumbled along, I'd watch through the window seeking out familiar landmarks, just to make sure we were on the right route headed for Wounded Knee, east toward the sun. We'd ride through the village of Pine Ridge; pass by fields dotted with cows and horses to the turn off road; then up its winding path, over bumpy ruts to the peak of the hill, where I'd start straining to catch a glimpse of the roof of our home. The bus would round the curve to the right and head down the long stretch to the little green store, the Wounded Knee Trading Post, where people from the community were gathered waiting.

One elderly lady, Leslie Fast Horse, always stood with her hands clasped in front her: Her eyes sparkled and her smile was one of the warmest I've ever known. As soon as we were off the bus, she'd always say in Lakota "You're back!" reaching out to pat each of us on the shoulder. Her greeting would mark the end of speaking English. Then the others who had gathered would greet us and call out "Run home now!" We'd take deep breaths of the clear fresh air, filled with the scent of plum blossoms and run for home, throwing away all our papers as we went to rid ourselves of all reminders from that miserable place. Mom always waited on the porch of our two-room home, wearing an apron and would have food cooked, ready to fill us up. Home was comfortably warm and welcoming—no English spoken, no questions asked about school. Our summer days were filled with contentment, as we were surrounded once again by a community of people who cared for each other and shared with each other.

Year after year, though, summer dragged to the same sad ending. When the chokecherries were just about gone, the dreaded morning would arrive. Leslie Fast Horse and the people from the community would gather again at the store to wait with us for the yellow bus. There was no happy chatter, no storytelling, no smiling—just silence broken only by an occasional cough, the creak of a board or the shuffle of a foot, and faces without expression, eyes staring forward.

I always felt sick to my stomach on those mornings. Mom would give us a bit of her hard-to-come by money to take for Saturdays, but that money wasn't important, I just wanted to stay home. I didn't want to get on that bus. I dreaded where it would take me. A faint rumbling sound would break the silence. The bus approached, it's tires crackling over small pebbles lying on the dirt road, brakes squeaking, doors opening with a thud.

As I'd step onboard, all the warmth that had filled my heart throughout the summer vanished. Other children would be sitting in there, dressed in their best clothes, clutching writing tablets with big Indian heads pictured on the covers. Throughout the ride, girls would be sobbing and the boys would sit silently with their heads down to hide their tears. When we'd pull up at the school, the bus door would open and the smell of newly cut grass would overpower us. It made me feel sick. All the children in the bus and on the school grounds were quiet. It would take some three weeks to break that silence. Gradually, we'd start pretending to be happy, to lift our spirits up, but the only true joy was felt in the excitement of going home.

Every time we returned to school from summer break the matrons would make us take our clothes off. They'd carry a whip or a stick. We'd stand naked as they tossed school clothes at us. We were given two sets to last for the year and only allowed to change them once a week. Our clothes from home were put away in boxes.

Many kids would carry small bits of things clutched in their hands when they returned to school, precious reminders of home—a bit of string, a piece of bread, a rock, food, or a shoelace. Some of the kids carried those bits and pieces in bags; others hid them in their shoes or socks and put them in their pockets later. Whenever the teachers caught a child, they would march him over to a trashcan and make him throw those things away; he wouldn't be allowed to eat as punishment. The boys who didn't get caught would always sneak back food for the others who had been punished.

I didn't understand at first, but as time went on, I started carrying items like that too. I remember how it felt to be marched to that trashcan. My hand would tighten around my treasure and when I released its hold, I'd mourn the loss of that tiny piece of home.

We comforted each other in the Lakota manner as best we could. We'd speak the Lakota language, which uses tone of voice and choice of words differently than English. It came out naturally and we didn't recognize the difference until years later. Sometimes we'd sneak off and find an isolated area, like the storm drain, in which to speak. Other times, a nod of the head, eye contact, or a brush on the arm would let another boy know he wasn't alone. When a boy was called into the office, it was common knowledge that meant a whipping was in store for him. We'd wait silently outside the door and move off to the side as he came out, tears running down his face. By our presence, we'd comfort. There was a room the older boys would talk about in a hushed way. It was empty. They told us stories of boys locked in there because of something they never had done.

The adults—teachers, matrons, the Boys' Advisor—repeatedly asked us questions about our family life. "Does your mother wash your clothes?" "Do you bathe at home?" "Do your mother and father bathe?" "Do your parents speak English?" "Did your mother go to school?" "Did your father go to school?" "Do your parents work?" We didn't know how to respond. Their voices were so curt and harsh, we were afraid to answer. Then they'd press—"Tell the truth! Don't lie!"—making us feel scared and ashamed.

Reading became my favorite activity. Through stories like "The Adventures of Tom Sawyer", I could glimpse freedom. By fourth grade, I was able to read fast and answer any questions given to me about the book I was reading. Again and again, the teacher would insist that I must have cheated and she would order me to sit off by myself.

I remember a boy named Tony who slept across the aisle from me. He was about six or seven years old when he got sick, bent over in pain. They took him to the hospital and after five or six days he came back, moving slower, his face pale. No adult came to watch after him, just the boys in the room. One evening, after getting ready for bed, we made eye contact and I felt a lot of pain radiating from him. A couple of hours later some adults came after him and that was the last I saw him. A day later, we learned that Tony had died. His appendix had burst, so he couldn't have survived.

One time, I got sick at school and was feverish. I stayed in bed for three days. The other boys brought me food. I couldn't walk. My brother Ben visited twice a day. At night when I fell asleep, I felt as if I were falling, tumbling, my body would be covered in sweat. I'd feel a bit better when the sun came up. During the day, adults would pass by my bed without stopping. On the third day, as everyone was getting ready for bed, a big boy came and carried me out to a car. The Boys' Advisor drove me to the hospital, where I stayed for two weeks. Another boy, Lester Young Dog, was in the room with me. He kept vomiting, I never learned why; but sharing that experience created a lifelong bond between us.

Another time, a boy was sitting on the second-floor window ledge reading a book. He turned the wrong way and fell to the ground. No adults came to his aid; only the boys responded. He came back up the stairs with his shoes untied, limping, tears running down his cheeks. The Boys' Advisor looked at him and said, "You're okay. Go to bed." Later he got whipped for the accident. He limped for a long time. Boys were punished for things like that. It was said they did it to stay out of class.

No matter what we did we got punished. Aside from beatings and whippings, we'd be made to wash windows, clean bathrooms, scrub floors and pick up trash. Sometimes, the Boys' Advisor would decide a particular punishment hadn't been enough and he would call on the older high school boys to form a line. I've heard it called a gauntlet. They'd stand in a straight line with their legs spread and the little boy being punished had to crawl through. As he crawled, they'd beat him with straps and sticks. Sometimes the Boys' Advisor would get angry with an older boy for not hitting hard enough.

I remember a day when we were in the third grade. Our teacher jerked a boy named Scooter out of his desk so roughly the desk fell over. Then he was hit with a book. I remember the shock and fear I felt so clearly. Scooter fell to the floor. I saw dust fly out of his pants; he was grabbed by the collar and yanked up to his feet. He had to pick up the desk and move it to sit in the corner facing the wall. I think he might have been talking.

Three brothers from Manderson were brought to school in the middle of the year. They cried all day to go home and followed each other around. We'd talk to them, but they'd just shake their heads. The matron told them to "Shut up! Stop crying! Be quiet!" You could tell they were close, for they never strayed far from each other. The oldest always tried to care for the other two. They slept in different rooms because of their ages. The one in our room cried every night. As soon as we could, we would talk to him, but if we were caught talking, we'd be punished. The middle one, Curtis, was soft-spoken and gentle, always there helping others with their problems, never focusing on himself. As an adult he became a medicine man. Yet, none of them were ever able to find relief from their memories of the cruelty they had experienced at boarding school. Curtis, overwhelmed by the painful memories, took his own life. All three are gone now.

By the middle of fifth grade, I decided I didn't want to go there anymore and I started running away. I'd run home, sixteen miles straight across country. One time two other boys came with me, and we hid out in an old shed. We ate berries and whatever else we could find. But the one boy didn't like it, and went home and pretty soon the other boy and I went home too. Sure enough, the car came and got us. After a few escape attempts, they kept me in jail at night for a week. I was placed in the women's section because I was so young. A tribal policeman would escort me to school every morning and chain my right arm to the desk. Even then, I got hollered at for being late one day.

    Still I ran. I clearly remember the last time I ran away. It was in the winter and six to eight inches of snow lay on the ground with deep drifts. I grabbed four candy bars that I had stashed away and just started running. I followed the road but tried to stay just off to the side so I could hide if need be. I stumbled in the drifts. My shoes kept falling off because they were too big, but still I kept going. I wasn't even aware of the cold. I was so intent on getting home. Six or seven hours later, well after dark, I made it. No one was home so I hid in the root cellar. One of my older brothers found me there and carried me inside. My feet had become so swollen I couldn't walk. I remember the care my mother and my brothers gave to me while I lay in bed recovering. My brothers gathered wood for the stove to keep the house warm. They carried me to and from the outhouse and gave me food to eat before they'd eat theirs. They were constantly checking my feet.

    Three or four days went by when, late one night, the tribal police came to take me back. I remember lying on my bed in the dark, hearing them arrive. I knew I couldn't run any more. I couldn't even walk. I remember so clearly the firmness in my mother's voice—not rage, not anger—it was a tone filled with power. Her words were very clear and simple, "No, you will not." In that moment, my whole being was flooded with overwhelming relief and the fear in me vanished.

    Over the following days, relatives and neighbors stopped by the house. Some brought food, a bowl of soup, pieces of fry bread, even cloth. There was a lot of handshaking. Their words of encouragement, sharing and caring, and depth of compassion filled our home. My mother's moral courage and resolve to protect gave me courage and provided some emotional balance to the horrors I had experienced at the government boarding school. For a short time after that, I was sent to stay at Holy Rosary, the

Catholic boarding school, but it seemed to me the atmosphere there was no different.

Even today, all these years later, when I drive near those schools my head throbs and I feel sick to my stomach. The old boys' dormitory at OCHS, with its big crack from the ground to the roof, boards holding it together, is gone. New buildings have replaced it. It seems to me those school buildings, and even the land around them, are embedded with frustration, resentment, anger, and hate—almost as if they are haunted. When I occasionally need to return, everything inside of me shuts down. Those places represent hell to me. The people in authority thought the schools were good because their job was to civilize us and mold us into acceptable human beings. They were meant to be institutions of learning, but were instead institutions of destruction. The legacy of Henry Pratt lived on: "Kill the Indian, Save the Man." We were beaten and punished to instill a different way of life that we didn't understand nor want, and we were taught behaviors that we should never use in our life.

I don't think we ever experienced how to be carefree boys or girls. When many of us became teenagers and young men, the boarding school experiences stayed within us as anger and frustration. We had a hard time expressing ourselves. Some of my former classmates committed suicide, some drank themselves to death, and others just gave up and didn't care whether they lived or died.

Those of us who have tried to carry on have found little on the reservation to give meaning to our lives. We have developed unique behaviors to survive. Our conversations tend to be guarded, and we frequently withdraw and fade into the background in a crowd, rarely stepping forward to participate. We cut conversations short just to get away from others; we tend to be suspicious of people, meetings and group activities. For many of us there are no feelings of freedom, or pleasure. There is nothing. We are just there, silent observers of our own lives. We feel a need to be close, but just "close by," not really involved.

Throughout my life, I have never forgotten when I was that little five-year-old boy staring out from behind my brother at a familiar stranger and the vow I made to always remember my mother. Her strength and determination have been the greatest guiding light in my life. Her light has beckoned to me throughout the most trying and confusing times; when I have felt hopeless and alone. The firmness in her voice, while I lay in bed on that night the police came, still resounds in my ears.

CHAPTER SEVEN

Culture Shock

I had survived seven years at OCHS before my mother was allowed to transfer me over to another boarding school, the Holy Rosary, run by the Catholic Church in Pine Ridge. For a year I struggled within its oppressive confines, not feeling any relief. I lived day by day in a dark fog, governed by stern men in long black robes. Finally, whether through a change in laws or circumstances, I don't know, my mother was able to get me transferred again—to the community public school, run by the state of South Dakota—just yards from our home. I went there for two years, graduated from the eighth grade and quit.

I stayed at home for another two more years, with a lot of time on my hands, little to do. Our world on the reservation had become more or less meaningless. There was no place to go, nothing meaningful to do, no movies, no library, no public transportation, no jobs available to make a decent life—just the manual labor of harvesting crops. I felt there had to be a better way of life. I dreamed of finding something I could do to gain skills that would be useful to help myself, and the others who were living here. Eventually, I learned of a vocational training program offered by the Bureau of Indian Affairs (BIA) in San Francisco. In search of a better way of life, I took advantage of the opportunity. Two months after my seventeenth birthday, in 1959, I left the reservation to go to San Francisco to attend a vocational training program in cabinetmaking.

My mother's brother, my Uncle Ben, came by to brief me on what to expect as I moved from rural life to life in the city. There was really little he could share, though, as Uncle Ben had never lived that far from Pine Ridge. I had heard about the different experiences from my brothers had had when they served in the armed forces and were away from home, but nothing I had heard really prepared me for things like running water in the home, electricity, telephones, trolley cars, and Laundromats.

I had butterflies in my stomach as I boarded a train at midnight in Alliance, Nebraska. I was both scared and excited to be traveling to a foreign place and seeing different parts of the country. It was my first train ride. I had seen trains but had never ridden in one. I wondered how I was going to get through all this and survive. The train stopped in Sydney, Nebraska where we had to get out and board another train that took us to Denver, Colorado. In Denver, the conductor explained to me that they would change engines but not the train. From there it was a ride clear through to Oakland, California.

I had just gotten used to the smells and sounds of the train, but getting off in the city, I was confronted with a whole new mix. The people looked different, sounded different, and smelled different. The heat of Oakland, its noise and people moving quickly, felt very strange. I couldn't understand their way of talking—it was neither unfriendly nor friendly—the noise simply didn't make any sense. Feelings I thought I had left at boarding school resurfaced. Once again, I felt fearful and isolated.

Following a set of written directions, I took a bus to San Francisco. Crossing the Bay Bridge, I saw the tall buildings of the city. There was no color, nothing that made a person feel good. Once off the bus, I entered the station and asked the attendant for a taxicab. I remember that taxi ride, how I spied crowds of people on Market Street and wondered, "Where are all these people going? Where do they live? Where do they eat? Where do they sleep?"

The cab dropped me off at a "residential" that provided a bedroom, a dining room and a gathering room with a television. I lived there with twenty-five other people, whom I saw only when it was time to eat. Still, it was a good enough place.

The following morning I continued to follow the written instructions and walked about fifteen blocks to the Bureau of Indian Affairs office. The old feeling of having to go to the Boys' Advisor at boarding school to receive punishment came back to me as I walked through the door into the office. The treatment I received was actually very similar. I was told curtly where to go, where to sit, how to dress, how to act, and to speak "fluent English." They gave me a check for my clothing allowance and a paper listing the names and addresses of recreational places for weekends—like the Arthur Murray Dance Studio. Directions were then given on how to get to the cabinet-making school—what bus number to take and where and how to get off the bus. Last, the BIA told me the name of the bank that would cash my stipend checks.

For the first month, I lived in the residential and then I moved into an apartment with a guy from Reno, Nevada. San Francisco—the feelings, the sights, the sounds, the smells, crowds of people, traffic, cars, and the noise—was overwhelming. I wanted to turn back, to go home, but there were no opportunities there, no future on the reservation. Soon I discovered stores that were open twenty-four hours a day, fast-food restaurants, buses, and different types of music. I discovered the ocean and beaches. I learned how to use a phone and laundry facilities. Here, I could take a shower every day, sit in front of a TV, or go see a movie.

Others like me were also in the city. Sometimes I went to the Indian Center and met up with young people from other reservations, mostly from the southwest: Apache, Navajo, Hopi and Ute. I ran into five Lakota, three from Pine Ridge and two from Standing Rock. They were all struggling to adjust too.

Most of us Indians were capable of learning quickly, and we'd try to find a humorous way around embarrassing situations. There was confusion over so many differences though. All of us had come from areas lacking the luxuries of San Francisco. The southwest Indians were so used to conserving water that it was hard for them to watch people use it freely. We had to learn about using washers—how to fill them, when and how to add the soap, and how to turn them on. I had never seen a dryer before. A lot of us were used to outhouses, and I'd watch some get up every morning and go outside to look around before it would dawn on them to go back inside the residential building.

It seemed to me that our lives had been so firmly shaped by the government boarding schools that we had difficulty making our own decisions. We were always expecting someone to come by and yell at us, and looked at every experience as if it were connected to some rule or regulation. We were always guarded, scared to reach out, and feared being punished. We'd wonder, "What's going on here?" "What are they up to?" We'd tell the residential manager when we were going out and when we would be returning, though day after day he'd say, "You don't have to tell me." Some of us would just stay in the TV room waiting for the manager to turn the set on or to give permission for us to touch the knobs on it; others would never go out except to go to the training. We were so afraid of stepping out of line. There was always that niggling thought that if you made one mistake, you'd be sent home as a failure and you'd lose face within your community.

Not knowing how to handle a situation, we'd often feel stupid, embarrassed and frustrated. To go into a restaurant with a lot of people was scary. We'd look for small cafés and settle for whatever they served. In the reservation border-town cafes, Indians were ignored and never served equally. The treatment in the city was unfamiliar and different. We were leery and suspicious, waiting for someone to yell, "Get back in line." It was a struggle to try to feel positive or good in any way. We didn't recognize that we were a part of the everyday crowd. Therefore, we always had that hesitation to step forward and join in.

At times, I would seek relief from the everyday city crowds and go to the Indian Center. It had a live band and dancing on Saturday nights. The dance floor was usually empty, while I would sit and hope somebody would have enough courage to get out on it. Usually a person would come by, tap me on the shoulder and pair me off with a girl. I'd dance with her in a stiff, awkward way, worrying all the while over what my partner thought. Was she disappointed in my style? Did she want to dance with someone else? No one else danced in a carefree way either. Freedom of expression was totally unknown to us.

Some of us would attend sporting events, but the crowds were intimidating. A lot of us from the reservations never reacted to the games. We just sat quietly in a guarded way for emotional responses had been killed in us.

We found a few ways to cope, sharing information with each other in order to overcome loneliness. If we found some place that was high—a building or a hill—we'd share how to get there and say, "Go and get lost," meaning, here's a place to escape the everyday confusion. Despite our common challenges, we Indians from the reservations didn't form strong, emotional attachments, but we acted more like distant friends, who never really visited with each other. Some got discouraged and returned to their reservations.

Many times, I'd sit by myself thinking about what the older people had told me. I enjoyed the experience of owning a radio and a wristwatch, and took pleasure in understanding how to dress. But even the idea of going out anytime of the day for a cup of coffee at a café or restaurant never really felt good, or natural, because it contrasted too much with the lives of the people back on the reservation and that made me feel badly. Despite everything that was available, I found no pleasure in learning. To survive I learned well what was taught. Operating table saws and different types of cabinetmaking machinery fell into my original plan to learn something I could take home to help the people there.

I finished the courses in 1961 just in time to join a declining job market for cabinetmakers. I had no place to use my newly found skills. I wasn't ready to return to the reservation and a lot of my friends, who were reservists, were being called into active duty. Therefore, I joined the army, hoping to catch up with them.

CHAPTER EIGHT

Losing Ground

When I enlisted in the army in September of 1961, I was unaware of the mental and emotional baggage I was carrying with me from boarding school. Only now, can I see and understand that burden more clearly. I often felt numb, almost paralyzed. At times, I would feel as if things around me weren't real. Then hate, bitterness and frustration would suddenly surface from deep within me, alarming me; I couldn't place what had triggered those feelings. It became easier to drink, get drunk, and stay drunk.

In the months between enlisting and being sworn in, I finished up school and got things in order. The director of the school had told me I could consider leaving early and he would send my certificate to Wounded Knee, but I lingered in San Francisco until Christmas. I called in to the army the day after New Year's in 1962 and was told to report to a hotel in Oakland.

They provided food tickets and a list of places to eat. At five-thirty the next morning, I was given a wake-up call to report to the induction center at seven. There a group of us were tested, given a physical exam and an oath to repeat. A bus took us to Fort Ord, California, at three in the afternoon. I felt excited but had a knot in my stomach, experiencing the familiar boarding-school fear. Had I done the right thing? The other guys were whooping it up, laughing, but I sat off to the side, unable to join in.

It was well into the night when we pulled into Fort Ord. The bus door swung open. A large uniformed man entered and everyone got quiet. He looked around and spat out one word: "Shit!" We were driven to the reception area where another fellow with stripes on his sleeve boarded a now very quiet bus. He yelled: "Get out, line up facing the building. You're going to eat, then run to the building you're assigned to. Pay attention. You're in the Man's army now!"

Once again in my life, my hair was cut off. We lined up and were measured for uniforms, underwear, and socks. At the end of the line, a sergeant told us to change and put our civilian clothes in a box to donate to charity or to send home. I felt so intimidated by the loss of my hair. Even though the uniforms fit much better and felt more comfortable, I felt like I was in school again.

We went back to the barracks and were told when it would be time to eat. After a few days, they called out names and gave us directions over a loudspeaker. We were to carry all of our clothes and bedding; we were to leave the mattress folded to one end of our bed. We were placed on buses, taken to a modern building, and were assigned to platoons. Drill instructors lined us up and told us where to put our things. There was to be no talking. In formation, we marched to a supply room and were issued rifles, helmets, and canteens. Drill instructors lined us up, barking out orders to put our things into wall lockers in military fashion. We were told to keep our surroundings and ourselves clean, that discipline was a key part of a proud man. In the back of my mind, I worried, wondering how I would be punished if their standards were not met. What would happen to me?

I struggled to remind myself that I was a young adult, not a child. Over the next ten weeks of boot camp at Fort Ord, I gradually became aware of differences with the boarding school experience. No one hit, whipped, or kicked us. The hollering was even different, intended to accomplish an objective—to encourage, although at a loud level—rather than to degrade. The supplies of food, clothing, and bedding, were much better than those at boarding school. Some complained constantly about the walking and running while carrying a heavy weight and about how often we had to clean. I couldn't understand them, feeling in myself something like pride because of our contribution to the welfare of the elderly, the children, and the land. I was determined to complete the military service to the best of my ability.

We were given leave after boot camp and I had made plans to visit my mother. When I arrived at the train station in San Francisco, two military policemen (MP's) approached me. The fear in my stomach was so cold that I didn't hear them at first. Checking my name against a list, they told me that there had been a "change of orders"—I was to go to Presidio. Once again, I found myself in another reception area, complete with a building for eating and one for sleeping. I recall the WACs (as the women in the army were called), serving the food, yelling out catcalls and whistling, at the men. I had never seen that behavior before in women. Their lack of dignity was embarrassing to watch.

I was soon assigned to the Fifth Mechanized Division, reactivated by President Kennedy at Fort Carson in Colorado Springs, Colorado. For the first time in my life, I flew in an airplane. The window seat provided a new, freeing perspective of the land. I landed in Colorado Springs feeling apprehensive, lost, and lonely. Surprisingly, a stranger offered me a ride to the bus station and all along the way people were helpful. At Fort Carson, a smiling, black man, Hudson, introduced himself to me and shook my hand. I had never met a black person before, and the two of us were the only occupants of the barracks that first night. We were ordered to clean out the whole building, a huge task since it had last been used as a World War II internment camp for Japanese Americans. The dirt lay four inches deep. The windows were dirty—some were without panes—and it was cold, the old barracks heated only by a coal fire. Even with all we did to clean it up, it was still a barren, open area, similar to the reservation, dusty, dreary, and depressing.

Over the next two weeks, 25,000 GIs arrived, an amazing sight, and by the end of the month, 55,000 troops were stationed at Fort Carson. They came from New York, Georgia, North Carolina, Virginia, Florida, Ohio, and one from South Dakota. The troops from the east were very different, complete with confusing accents and had freer behavior than I had experienced. The New Yorkers were friendly, but those from the southern states would ignore me, reminding me of the treatment we Indians had gotten in the small towns bordering the reservation.

We were molded into a combat-ready mobile fighting unit, trained in chemical, germ, and guerilla warfare tactics. We were taught battlefield first aid. We developed physical endurance through swimming, running, and living off the land. Military life was acceptable much like what my brothers had described, but I struggled to sort out my own thoughts and deal with insecurities and fears.

Although my life now seemed to have little connection to home, thoughts and memories of the reservation kept surfacing. I sent fifty-five dollars of my sixty-five dollar monthly pay home to my mother. I desired to accomplish something, to be proud of my life, to feel well and whole and to grow. At times I did achieve success through letters of commendation received in training, marching, map reading, and marksmanship. Still the dread of recognition and being singled out for punishment lingered.

They Called Me Uncivilized

Many of the guys were willing to be friends and were quite curious about my life and Lakota culture, but I found it difficult to reciprocate. They wanted to know if we still wore feathers. And, did we live in tipis? Or, did we ride horses? What food did we eat? Did we still scalp or steal people? I couldn't talk openly, even to guys who were sincerely interested, because all I could see was the reservation's poverty. In contrast, others freely chatted about their homes, cars, things they owned, schools, social life, restaurants, and nightclubs. East Coast towns had fancier sounding names; even the Bronx sounded better than Wounded Knee. I felt embarrassed to talk about my culture and the boarding school. It seemed easier to withdraw, remain detached and be a loner. I didn't try to make any close connection with others from Pine Ridge when we would meet up at the Cheyenne Club or other places downtown. There was only one from the reservation I connected with, Wilbur Between Lodges. Perhaps it was because Wilbur always has had a warm, gentle smile and a relaxed friendly nature, which brings out the best in a person.

I was undeniably part of Indian Country, yet I preferred not to be. Once a busload of Indian people came from Cheyenne, Wyoming, to perform at Fort Carson's social club. The captain granted me permission to go and excused me from duty. Dressed in full uniform, I saw guys dancing whom I had gone to school with. They were dressed in our traditional dancing outfits made with fancy beadwork and wore moccasins on their feet. As I watched them, I kept thinking, "I'm different from them." I stayed seated, not wanting to talk to the dancers or participate. I hesitated on whether to leave or stay. An elderly woman, in her seventies or eighties, approached me. She shook my hand and spoke to me in Lakota. Her name was Blue Star. I sensed pride coming from her, but I wasn't able to respond in a respectful way. I wanted to say, "Don't talk in Lakota," so I replied to her in English. Nevertheless, she said, "You are Lakota," and I stiffened in resistance to her words. For years, I have been intensely ashamed of my disrespect, my ignorance, my rejection of Blue Star and the dancers. But, I couldn't make it right. I couldn't find the people to apologize to, to ask forgiveness from them. I live with those memories and that deep regret.

I started drinking heavily, forgetting the advice from the older Lakota, my uncles, brothers and mother. It was as if I threw my heritage away. Alcohol supplied relief, not pleasure. I'd first hold my breath to avoid tasting it, then once slipping into it, I didn't have to think or worry. I would go right into drunkenness. I wasn't a social drinker and didn't realize I was abusing my body, mind and emotions, fooling myself, spending more of my free time getting drunk. It's easy to fool yourself when you're drunk.

Drinking wrapped comfortably around my responsibilities to the army. I kept up my appearance as a good soldier is supposed to do—boots always polished, uniform pressed with sharp creases, and sleeping area spotlessly clean. I fed and cleaned the cage of "Caisson," a bobcat that was the company's mascot. I got money to support my drinking by setting some aside after buying necessities and picked up extra change by taking guard duty for others. How smart I was to figure this out, the good soldier who controlled drinking by just following a plan.

In October of 1962, the Cuban Missile Crisis placed the base on Red Alert. The atmosphere was tense; we expected a nuclear war to break out and couldn't reason what role we could play against a bomb of such magnitude. For approximately thirty days we waited to be transported to Miami, Florida, constantly wearing our full combat gear, including firearms, ammunition, and equipment. We weren't allowed to leave the base and had to be ready to leave for war at a moment's notice. Our whereabouts were reported at all times, even when using the restroom or taking a shower. The mess hall was open twenty-four hours a day and only seven people were allowed to eat at a time. Four guards were placed on the corners of our block with orders to shoot anyone who stepped outside the boundaries. All entrances to the fort were shut down, and we were restricted to our barracks. We were afraid, fearful from not being able to communicate with our families and friends, fearful from not knowing when or how war would come. The stress affected some severely, and two were taken to a hospital.

When it was over, and we returned to our normal army routine, I couldn't quite get back into focus or fully concentrate. The army had lost its appeal and never again held its special meaning for me. Even though I continued to do what was expected of me, I didn't like the place anymore and wanted to leave.

Over the next two years, the army sent me for training in Arizona, Nevada, California, North and South Carolina, Georgia, the state of Washington and overseas to Germany. Talk of a conflict in Southeast Asia, Vietnam, surfaced increasingly in news reports. A lot of GIs claimed, that if it came to war, they'd go without being asked. I listened to the talk and looked at Vietnam as an escape from the boredom of where I was stationed. A recruiting sergeant offered assurances that I could be sent there on temporary duty. For a while, I tried to imagine what it would be like to face death if need be, wondering if my death might impact upon anyone. However, those thoughts were empty of any emotions for, at this point in my life, nothing really mattered or appealed to me. I was certain my mother would mourn, but I couldn't even summon up that mental image to attach feelings to. Finally, I made my decision to go based on a phrase I had often heard at boarding school—"You do it because you're supposed to"—and I applied.

Any emotions I had left in me, I could easily push back knowing that they wouldn't do me any good. I had already learned that well in boarding school—I used those lessons all of the time. It wasn't even a conscious thought; it was part me. I simply did what I was "supposed to do."

I felt no glory, no honor, no pride in the orders I carried out; I had no thoughts of protecting the land, the elderly, or the children. The survival lessons I had learned as a boarding school child had strengthened over the years and overshadowed any memories of summers I had spent among the compassionate elders of the Wounded Knee community. The six months I spent in Vietnam on temporary duty was a blur.

In April of 1965, I received an honorable discharge for my service. I was tired from all my experiences and returned to the reservation, to Wounded Knee. After seven years of education, traveling in the army and living among foreigners and I still had no self-confidence though I longed for it. Worse, I felt like a stranger within my community, even when I visited with my brothers and my mother. It seemed impossible to talk to or to get close to anyone. I struggled with numerous attempts at friendship, tried many different relationships, but all were short-lived.

It was easier to drink, to get drunk and to stay drunk. When I was sober, I had no feelings, I was numb to life and would just go through the motions every day. I went from job to job, mostly involving physical labor, such as seasonal farm work—or whatever would get me a paycheck at the end of the week so I could get drunk and find relief from the dark fog that lay within. Yet, the relief and pleasure from drinking were short-lived; I'd feel a little joy, a little pleasure. However, alcohol leads to carelessness and I'd forget that it would trigger a cold rage that lay just below the surface. Within minutes of taking a drink, I would begin to look for a fight using the smallest reason I could find to blame. Any friendships I formed were always based on getting alcohol; who had a bottle; who had money; how we could get it. As soon as the alcohol was gone, we'd split up and go our separate ways. My life centered on alcohol, and its ability to bring me a brief moment of pleasure. All together, I drank for thirteen years.

Looking back now, after more than thirty sober years, my memories of that time of indifference still appall me. Yet, that's what happened to many of us who were tortured as children; we sought relief through alcohol or drugs. Our ability to feel and to be human had been taken away.

CHAPTER NINE

Our Own Worst Enemy

I lived in that darkness for eight more years, from 1965 through 1973, until there came a turning point. My mother was aging and had moved out of her small WPA home into HUD's public housing located on the other side of the massacre site. It eased life a bit for her to have a place with indoor plumbing. She had a small monthly income from Social Security. I often visited her, my uncle and other relatives. We Lakota had always visited with each other, sometimes staying for days at a time.

The political system on the reservation had become completely corrupt. It seemed to me nothing was being done for the majority of the people. Little help was available, not even for the elderly or the children, unless a person was related to a member of the Tribal Council or the president of the tribe. It was common knowledge that job openings weren't filed by people who needed work but by the politicians' relatives. People were kept in line through intimidation and threats of incarceration.

Our original form of leadership had been organized around a system of group agreement. It consisted of the headsmen from each Tiyospaye (extended family) working together to make decisions on matters that concerned the whole group. Each Tiyospaye created its own day-to-day lifestyle with a headman and his wife handling conflicts and making decisions within it. It was a system based on group consensus that generated harmony, respect, and honor. The strength of the group depended on the unique talents of the individuals within it. However, in 1934, the authority of the Tiyospaye was replaced through the Indian Reorganization Act, a foreign system in which elected "officials" made decisions and the everyday person's voice was no longer heard.

Newly elected representatives no longer tried to figure out what was positive for the people. Instead, they looked for what was best for the tribal council's agenda and their own financial gain. They learned how to speak in double-talk, how to maneuver political power plays, how to make hollow promises, how to use police intimidation to force the everyday people to toe the line. It was a totalitarian state—not a democracy by any means. Through it, the political group leading the reservation took control by assuming absolute authority in total disregard for our way of life.

So-called bodyguards, who were openly vocal, harassing and intimidating people, protected the Tribal President. As time went on, he began having them hired as police officers. In turn, they started forming their own groups, known as goon squads. Anyone who opposed the Tribal president was assaulted and or incarcerated. A reign of terror spread across the reservation.

In February of 1973, more confusion was added to the mix. My brother Wilson had been in the hospital and Ben and I had picked him up and brought him back to our mother's house.

Early the following morning a stranger rode up to the house and told us that we could get food at the Wounded Knee Trading Post and any bills we owed would be taken care of. He said we should go over there and get whatever we wanted. Ben and I didn't understand what he was talking about and went over to see. At the trading post, we saw people pushing carts around and we learned that a group called the American Indian Movement (AIM) had taken over the community during the night. They occupied the Catholic church on the massacre site hill and we heard they had taken the storeowners as prisoners. On the third or fourth day shooting started, and we realized our community was in an armed takeover. We didn't learn the reason for ten more days; AIM had come to remove the Tribal President from office.

Soon, the Wounded Knee community was also surrounded by U.S. marshals, who blocked all the roads. Many of us were confused and frightened and lacked information. We'd walk to the Trading Post to learn more, keeping to the ditch because of the shooting. We didn't know if or when we would be shot at. It seemed every time we turned around someone was pointing a gun at us. Several times, we hiked up to the church seeking information from AIM, but they wouldn't let us in or talk to us. We were caught in the middle; neither side seemed to be considering our welfare or security.

Many times AIM members threatened to shoot us. Despite their public statements saying that local residents were to be left alone, we all experienced bullying from them. They came from a lot of different nationalities and some were mixed with Indian. I don't think any of them cared or realized what life was all about. I saw them imitate and copy what they thought a Lakota was to be, but they had a complete lack of respect and they spoke in city street slang, which had no pride. It was embarrassing to watch and listen. None showed any Lakota behavior that we were familiar with. Their actions were more like those of gangsters.

They always hollered about "The Cause! We're doing this for The Cause!"

They dressed with feathers and a little beadwork here and there. Their hair was braided and held into place with headbands, whereas the men in our community wore more of a casual, everyday western style, which fit the weather conditions. They screamed and hollered about being Indian, yet, here we Lakota were living right in front of them in a quiet respectful manner; they didn't seem to see us.

Randolph Sun Bear, Solomon Bear Eagle, and I watched them lead a cow in one day. As a group of them were just standing around looking at it, one of the local residents went over and inquired what they intended to do with it. They replied that they were going to butcher it, yet they didn't even know how to kill it. The local told them to shoot it between the eyes and watched in surprise as one AIM member pulled out a small pistol, stood six feet away, took aim and fired six times. The cow still stood. Then the local told them to use a rifle with heavier ammunition and shoot from a closer range. Finally, the cow was dead, yet they still stood looking at it. At this point, several of us were watching out of curiosity. Again, the local told them to cut the jugular vein and let it bleed, then skin it, quarter it, and use every part. We left for a while but soon went back. The cow was still lying there. They still didn't understand what to do and none of them had any skinning knives or sharpening stones to carry out the process. With that, we realized they didn't know anything about what it takes to survive in this area and began to understand just how dangerous they were to themselves.

I had the impression these were just a bunch of little bullies. Even the way they greeted each other showed no respect, honor or pride. It was more like a show in which they had little parts to play. They traveled in groups of four or five intimidating people and using language that wasn't directed at anyone, not at the people in the community or at the federal marshals. They made it clear they would shoot anyone.

What disappointed me at that time was to hear the members of AIM holler, "This is a good day to die!" However, when the shooting started they'd run and hide, even pushing women out of the way. They did not attempt to protect even their own members.

After a few days, I began to see different Lakota coming in from other parts of the reservation. I could always pick them out. They were more sincere, extending their hands in a decent handshake, whereas the outsiders—the AIM members—went through a whole display like that of gang members. It was embarrassing.

We Lakota felt like we were being held captive. Roads were blocked. People were scared of being hit by a stray bullet or hurt by the disrespectful behavior of AIM members.

Living conditions became worse for the residents. Food supplies were nearly gone. Sometimes AIM members brought over food to the residents, but the meat they brought was obviously leftover scraps that were of little use. The canned goods were badly damaged. A lot of the people just didn't know what to do or what to think. We were concerned for each other and shared meals among ourselves. I saw people give one AIM leader cigarettes and other items, but I never saw him share them, not with his members nor with the people in the community. As Lakota, we were used to sharing everything equally, especially during hard times, and watching this behavior left very uncomfortable, bitter feelings in us. Someone drained the propane gas from the main tank that supplyed fuel to the all the homes in the housing area. People were no longer able to heat their homes or cook on their stoves. Many began cooking outside and moved into their basements to keep warm.

Homes were looted and ransacked. Residents who had run out of supplies started leaving, while others, who had been outside the area when the takeover began, were prevented from returning by roadblocks. Both groups eventually came back only to find their homes empty, ransacked, and looted. I personally witnessed my Uncle Ben's house burning down. AIM members were running out to a parked blue van. A nest had lodged in the chimney so I figured they had probably started a fire in the stove without checking the pipes. Our family home was completely ruined, torn up, its roof caved in. I found boards from it lining bunkers along with our woodstove. My mother's storage barrel had been turned over and all its contents stolen--her flute, beadwork, family photographs, and my cheap camera, and army uniform. Even her cast iron kettle was gone.

Then they left.

We were devastated. No trading post, no post office, no bridge, wrecked churches and homes. The wooden bridge leading to Porcupine was weakened because AIM had set a car on fire, to burn the bridge and keep the U.S. marshals out. Traffic couldn't pass over it anymore. Just about every home, except those in the HUD lower housing unit, had been looted, vandalized, and or destroyed beyond being repaired. The Catholic church was so shot up that the federal marshals declared it unsafe; even from a distance you could see the bullet holes in it. The Episcopal church, one of the original churches, was burned to the ground. The Presbyterian church had been vandalized and chopped up and was bullet-ridden. Even the Church of God's place of worship, which was off to the side, had bullet holes in it, but not as many as the others.

The federal marshals came in to inspect the area for safety, not knowing what AIM had left behind. No one was allowed to come back until their home had been checked. After the inspection, some people were allowed into their homes, but were told not to use their stoves. Individual propane tanks were brought in for houses. The marshals cautioned against wandering, since AIM might have planted landmines. Curiously, during that time, all the vehicles in the community were ordered to be removed. We don't know who gave that order. A couple of people lost their trailer houses and never got them back because they couldn't afford the towing charges.

From February to August 1973, our people had to live the best way they could with nothing. There was no running water, no heat, no electricity, no plumbing in any of the homes. Some people built outhouses with blankets and boards—whatever they could find. We used kerosene lamps and candles and everybody cooked outside. Many were missing everyday items like cooking pots and eating utensils. There often weren't enough plates or cups to go around for family members. For some, one cup might be used by all of them. One family had a broom's handle shot into two pieces, but they taped it back together as best they could to keep using it. We were hard pressed to find ways to get to Pine Ridge, seventeen miles away, for our mail and food. Water was hauled in plastic milk bottles, as people couldn't even find pails anymore. Personal hygiene was almost next to impossible during this time. Rumors flew that the water had been contaminated and so the marshals shut down the water for the housing area. All other wells were not to be used, except for the one up by the windmill. There were no more animals—no cats, no dogs, not even horses. Everything had disappeared.

The people in Wounded Knee depended on each other for help. Very little traffic passed through and most that did drove very fast. No visitors came from Porcupine because of the ruined bridge and those from Manderson traveled on another route to avoid us. The Red Cross came in for a short time to distribute sandwiches, cups of juice, and pieces of fruit. However, they left quickly because they feared being shot at. Members of the clergy and others feared for their lives and so stayed away.

Martial Law was declared after AIM was removed in early May. A curfew kept us inside from seven in the evening until eight in the morning; we were warned that anyone outside during those hours would be shot. Water was only available from a pump up near the Catholic Church where the windmill still stands, and we were told to follow the trail next to the tree line to get there. We were allowed to walk on only one road and had to stay in the center of it. Anything and anybody coming into Wounded Knee was checked. In some cases, if you brought in liquid, like Crisco oil, the marshals would dump it out just to make sure that nothing dangerous was smuggled in. Men, women and children were stripped down to be searched. I figured it was harder for women because all the marshals were men. It was embarrassing. These were acts that shouldn't take place in America. But, that's what went on at Wounded Knee.

All throughout that summer, we lived in fear that AIM would return and of retaliation by the tribal council and its goon-squad police force would retaliate. Several local people said they felt more protected by the U.S. marshals than by the Indian police. They treated us in a respectful way and would speak to us in a gentle manner seeking answers to questions they had. They occasionally provided transportation and in some instances ordered the tribal police out.

Now the feeling of what once was our Wounded Knee community was shattered, and homes and familiar landmarks were destroyed. Long-standing friendships and trust were replaced with suspicion and hopelessness. Nobody talked of the future. The community was divided into three factions: those for AIM, those for the tribal government and those who just wanted to continue on with their daily routines and survive as best they could. Yet no matter which we choose, we were left alone to deal with our own problems as no help came.

We heard a lot of rumors about financial and material donations earmarked for the community residents. Charitable organizations, groups of people, AIM and various individuals raised funds all across the world to help the Wounded Knee community get back on its feet, but to my knowledge the residents never received a penny of this money. The tribal council managed to divert the funds, even those left in wills, for their own interests. As to any money AIM raised, we understand it went into something called the Wounded Knee Defense Fund and used not to help the Wounded Knee residents but rather to pay off legal fees AIM had incurred. I know for a fact the Episcopal group accepted donations for us, but few of us received anything from them. All the donations were apparently under the control of the tribal president. To this day, donations earmarked for the Wounded Knee community most often get funneled into the governing body called the Wounded Knee District (whose headquarters is in the community of Manderson to the west), which usually informs us after the funds have been distributed. Checks have also been made out in error to The Wounded Knee Reservation, which have been cashed by the tribal government and never found their way to us.

The American Indian Movement, the Pine Ridge tribal government, the Bureau of Indian Affairs, and churches and charitable organizations all claimed to have helped the Wounded Knee community. In reality, the churches replaced their damaged buildings with new ones, but the clergy never developed any programs to address the deteriorated mental health and depression that the devastation had created in the people here. In reality, AIM, the tribal government and the BIA made promises to repair and replace homes, but words are like the wind—they come and go.

Across the reservation, "Wiping of the Tears" ceremonies were held along with other cultural honoring events. However, they always took place elsewhere, never in Wounded Knee. We were made to feel responsible for all that had taken place and were put in exile emotionally and physically from the rest of the people on the reservation.

During the whole takeover period, the noble words that guide many public service groups, "Protect and Serve," were manipulated to serve the interests of each separate group. They were never applied to the everyday people living in our tiny community. The Bureau of Indian Affairs never stepped forward to protect us. Its superintendent had U.S. marshals brought in to protect the BIA building. They were armed with machine guns and placed up on the roof with sandbags protecting them. The tribal council president and his goon squad certainly didn't have our protection in mind; in fact, they had begun to come down Wounded Knee Creek intending to eliminate everyone living here. However, the U.S. marshals stopped them at the Grooms place near the old wagon crossing.

AIM certainly didn't think of us. To them we were just a last-minute idea when their plans for the community of Calico fell through. No one warned us. No one asked us. No one stopped AIM from driving in. "Protect and Serve."

A few individuals, however, did come by, one by one, after it was over. They came from outlying towns and communities, Indian and non-Indian, everyday people, without much in the way of financial means. They came with compassion and courage, bringing food, candy and fruit, whatever they had, to help our children and families. They remembered us, those everyday people helping everyday people.

CHAPTER TEN

Remembering the Lessons from the Elders

Everything lay in ruins after the takeover; it was heartbreaking. Day after day, I'd walk around, counting the homes and buildings that were destroyed, left in shambles, looted, vandalized, burned. Gone were the homes of Cecelia Fast Horse, Helen and Silas Grant, Bill Cole, Mary Pike, Charlie Moose, Hobart Spotted Bear, Ben Iron Teeth, the High Pines, the Bear Eagles, Elmer Two Two, and my mother, Rosa. Gone were the churches many worshiped the Creator in, the Catholic, Episcopal, and Presbyterian, the trading post we had gathered in, and our museum. Gone was the laughter of children, along with the dogs, cats, and horses that had been our companions.

As I walked and counted buildings, I'd pass by friends and family members whose faces no longer sparkled with life or joy, their eyes averted and empty, shoulders hunched, heads cast down. Life felt completely hopeless. I thought I should feel rage, but instead I felt hollow, numb, and alone. At the age of thirty-one, I wanted—needed—to find a better way of life.

There was no help available on the reservation, no one to talk to, no one to turn to, certainly not from the government in Pine Ridge. Not even the priests and ministers came to help us heal. I knew that if I just focused only on what was negative, I'd kill myself; the pull toward suicide was strong.

One morning, there came a turning point. I hiked up the dirt trail to my father's homestead at Mouse Creek where my family had originally lived. I was looking for something with a little meaning that I could hold on to and get strength from. It was a pleasantly warm day. Songbirds were flitting in and about the trees lining the banks of the creek. Chokecherries were in season and wildflowers bloomed throughout the fields. A small flock of turkeys ambled in among the pines and deer stood on the south hill gazing down at me. I sat in the shade of the cottonwood for a long time, not even thinking, just giving myself over to the moment. Out of nowhere, I seemed to hear the word "remember." It jolted me. Where had it come from? What was I to remember? My eyes were drawn to that immense tree, and I felt a glimmer of hope.

Slowly, memories from my childhood began to come up to the surface. Voices of the elderly Lakota began to return to me in fragmented bits and pieces. I heard:

"Remembering is a basic ingredient for living."

"Remember to act these lessons out, and you will always have room in your mind for something new."

"All these things are part of being Lakota."

Slowly the voices faded and merged into images from my childhood. Once again I felt awe as I saw Good Lance appear before me, a round, brown, flat-brimmed hat on top of his head, his hair neatly held in two thick braids. He was dressed in his familiar purple silk shirt with the sleeves held in place by black armbands and wide leather cuffs laced over his wrists. A breach cloth was tied at his waist over the top of his pants and beaded moccasins covered his feet.

Then came Left-Handed Jimmy, the storyteller, wearing his black gabardine wool pants held up by thick, wide suspenders. As usual, he wore a small white Stetson, a light colored pinstriped shirt with armbands holding his sleeves, and the familiar large wristwatch flashed in the sunlight. I recalled how swiftly he walked, straight-backed, with a cane that never touched the ground.

As Jimmy's image faded, "Tall Charlie" Shot-to-Pieces appeared riding his horse. I remembered his distinctive style of speaking as he spoke English but thought in Lakota often putting the noun before the adjective like: "I came up on a fence two-wire." Although I never understood the way he used the word "to" in his sentences. I could still hear him saying: "walk to walk," "walk to run," "house to home."

Next, there was Lincoln Looking Horse in his long black coat that nearly touched the ground. Perched on his head was his black Scottish cap complete with a fur ball on top. Lincoln was a tall man with piercing eyes that drew you in and captured your attention. He had gone to Washington many times as a spokesman for us.

After Looking Horse, I saw Tall Jenny with her big pack on her back, a long ankle-length dress, and a scarf covering her hair. Her friendly face smiled at me once again, and I remembered how she'd travel from home to home giving out candy to the children.

I don't know how long I sat there hearing and seeing those people who had colored my childhood summers with their distinctive personalities and their loving ways, but suddenly a drumming sound brought me back to the present time. I looked around and spotted a small black and white speckled woodpecker with a red-capped head pounding and tapping on the side of the tree. In the stillness of that moment, I recalled one of the chief's words of advice—I don't remember which one it was—to the Lakota people and they seemed to take on an importance to me, as if in answer to my dilemma.

"Times have changed," he said. "You stand there saying that you have one foot in the red world and one foot in the white, unable to step forward. Take a little bit of the red and a little bit of the white, pull your feet together and step forward into the future."

The images and words that had come to me while I sat under the cottonwood tree, stayed in my mind as I left Mouse Creek. I recalled the impact those people had on me when I was young. You could sense every one of them come—like a rush of wind you knew they were there. Their personalities remained the same, unaltered no matter what the situation. You could hear them clearly without confusion. Even when they were all together, they didn't clash but rather created a sense of well-balanced power, respect, honor, and dignity. The way they talked, walked, and conducted themselves made you see them as dignitaries, which filled you with awe. In those moments, I had glimpsed the positive side of being Lakota and I was determined to draw it out from within myself. During the occupation, I had seen the blind leading the blind toward the destruction of Lakota wisdom.

The more I thought of the contrast between the members of the Wounded Knee occupation and the older Lakota, the more determined I became to create positive changes for myself. It took such effort to recall what words followed the fragments I had heard and to begin to put the pieces together. I had to slow way down in my thinking to sort out negative things I had learned and to attempt to get rid of them. I wish I could say it happened quickly, but it has taken me thirty years of remembering, applying common sense and struggling from that day to reach this point of understanding what it means to be Lakota, to be a human being, and to accept myself and find some peace.

Slowly, I realized my own spirit needed a good healthy home—a healthy mind and body. For the first time in thirteen years, I stopped drinking. I thought it would be the hardest thing, but it may have been the easiest, for even sober I was restless, tormented by dreams, thoughts and feelings and I'd clench my teeth to fight them down.

For years, I tried taking things one at a time in an attempt to redo myself. I would listen to what other people said, their tone of voice, choice of words, body language, manner of walking, style of dressing and I would mimic what I considered the best and try to make it a part of my everyday living. Yet still, I couldn't quite bring in feelings and emotions. I went from job to job, from relationship to relationship, and from place to place, taking pride in being sober.

Decades later, as I approached my sixtieth year, I began to realize, there was more to me, something was missing. Over the years, I had sought out lessons in Lakota spirituality, attended sweat lodges, prayed with others, sat on hills and sought visions. Yet, the other side of my childhood—nightmares from the government boarding school and beatings, overwhelming loneliness and resentment—seemed to take hold even stronger. Slowly, I realized the experiences in the government boarding school had kept me in a paralyzed place, where I couldn't seem to go forward, backward, or sideways. No matter what I had done for all those years, I still felt like a non-being, with my true self buried way down deep inside me.

At the age of sixty I was beginning to recognize what was triggering off those feelings and my reactions to them. As I looked around at my former classmates who were still alive, I started to become aware of the real cost of our survival and what was triggering such persistent terrible feelings and reactions. In such contrast to the strength in the faces of the elders of my childhood summers—Lincoln Looking Horse, Left-Handed Jimmy, Good Lance—I saw the faces of boarding school children reflected back at me, now lined with age. So many are still the silent observers; they withdraw and fade into the background of a crowd. There's a tired shyness in their smiles and, most often, they keep their eyes averted.

The contrast I saw in those faces got to me, I couldn't let them go. Morning after morning I sat at my kitchen table staring out at the immense cottonwood tree, very much aware of how old we both had become. Once more, I seemed to hear it say, "All things that ever happen are a part of today."

I sensed urgency in that moment to put together the pieces of our family history that I had gathered. Once more, I read my great grandmother, Iron Teeth's words. I thought of the laws, treaties, and agreements that had been written during her lifetime, taking away her freedom, which continue to have a strong impact on our reservation lives today. Over the generations, we have been restrained physically through the signing of the 1868 Fort Laramie Treaty and through acts of the U.S. Congress that further eroded our territory, in total disregard of the original agreement between our sovereign nations. During my grandparents' generation, our nation was again reorganized through the enforcement of the 1887 Allotment Act, which divided our land into family sections, eroding our communal way of life. It was confusing to people who never had conceived of possessing land since they were a part of the brotherhood of life.

Every generation in my family has been impacted by the laws of the U.S. Indian Courts, written in the 1800s, forbidding us to practice our spirituality and cultural traditions, forcing our people to pray, sing, and dance in hiding. Although we were finally given freedom of religion in 1979, much of our knowledge of traditional practices has been lost.

Competency laws in the early 1900s sought to divide my mother's brothers and sisters from each other according to the degree of "Indian blood" that ran through their veins. Through the imposition of those laws, which limited land ownership to competent people who were defined as those with more than one half "white blood," while those having "one half or more Indian blood" were automatically declared incompetent.

As I reviewed our history, I began to understand that with each generation, more and more confusion and frustration grew within the nature of our people. My family and others here have struggled under the impact of bewildering laws and the hardships created by extreme poverty to maintain dignity and respect for each other. Men like my father continued to send out the sound of our heartbeat through their drumming, a sound that creates courage and unity to all within its range.

As our history evolved into the present day, written laws have been manipulated from words on smooth paper into a cruel reality. We could survive land restrictions. We could hide and protect our spiritual beliefs. We could love each other regardless of blood degree. The ultimate destructive force, however, was the creation of the Indian boarding schools by the U.S. government in 1879. Through their policy, homes were emptied, communities mourned and all things Indian in a child were to be destroyed.

Iron Teeth never mentioned that her remaining son, White Buffalo, had been among those taken to the first boarding school, known as the Carlisle School. It was located in Pennsylvania and had been founded by Colonel Pratt under the motto, "Kill the Indian. Save the Man." Perhaps, like the generations who followed hers, Iron Teeth was unable to combat the horrific effects of the policy and felt it best not to speak of it. On the other hand, I have discovered that remembering and retelling is the path toward healing.

Like so many, I have lived a life blocked by fear, lead by fear, and governed by fear that was created in those childhood days.

Now I realize that the life I was forced to lead, the education, the experiences, the way I have come to look at things, the language I speak, all of it, has limited me because it wasn't a part of who I am, who I was born to be. Over time the cruelty inflicted upon me by the adults in the boarding schools had altered me from an innocent, smiling Lakota boy, a human being, to someone I no longer knew. Through their torture, I had become confused, bitter, and emotionally and psychologically crippled.

It hasn't been an easy task to set these memories down on paper. I have struggled for months and years to get them out. At times, I have wept, and at other moments, I've totally shut down. My doctor at the VA hospital urged me to keep trying to let the memories and emotions out. He told my wife, Jane, to let my reactions go over her head and not to allow my pain to enter her. It has been hard on both of us as we struggled along this memory path.

Finally, a breakthrough in my understanding came when I sought counsel from mental health professionals at the Victims of Violence program, in Boston, Massachusetts. They gave me the name of what I was suffering from—-Complex Post Traumatic Stress. It was immensely important to me, for once my fear had a name I could battle it and win. I learned that unlike Post Traumatic Stress Disorder, which comes from an event that has a clear beginning and end, Complex Post Traumatic Stress evolves when a person is tortured and abused for a very long time— months to years to generations. It is a natural emotional reaction to life-threatening, deeply shocking and disturbing experiences. When terrible things happen to us as children, as our personalities are still forming, the experiences change us, and they attempt to kill our ability to love, to care, to interact with other people, to express emotions in a positive healthy way, to be human. They attempt to kill our soul.

The fear created by the years of torture I had received in boarding school had attached itself to every aspect of my being.

Once I was armed with the words Complex Post Traumatic Stress, no longer was I battling an unknown enemy; with that knowledge, I started to see and hear more clearly. I began to recognize that things like the smell of freshly cut grass, the sight of a policeman, the stare of another person, or a curt tone of voice, automatically produce a response within me of re-experiencing feelings from boarding school. In those moments, I become resentful, confused, bitter, and mentally and emotionally crippled by a sense of overwhelming hopelessness.

With the knowledge of what triggers those feelings has come the awareness that I have power over it. It's still a struggle at times, but I am finally finding the freedom to be a human being. Sometimes I've forgotten the lessons and lost my way, but eventually I've remembered, felt bad, and tried all over again. In the process, I've learned how to maintain a stronger focus, to be more respectful in acknowledging other forms of life, to be a Lakota.

Through this process of remembering, I've become aware that the greatest help for healing has come to me through nature, starting with the cottonwood tree triggering positive memories. Slowly as I healed, I began remembering that we Lakota are a part of the brotherhood of life. I've recalled being taught by my Uncle Ben and other elderly people to pay attention to the behavior of the animals, the wind, the rain, the growth of trees and plants and the changes of seasons. The older Lakota were always reminding us to be grateful to and to respect the other forms of life here on earth. From lessons like that and others, my eyes were opened to see gifts from nature more often than we do now in this hurry-up day and time. I found wisdom from the animals that have helped me to realize and to understand how to use my own sense of hearing, eyesight, touch, taste, and smell.

From my life's experiences, it has been hard for me to find humor or to express it in that clear, pure way. The lessons our elders taught have taken me time to understand and often I've found myself straining to recognize their meaning. Often I'd remember hearing many different versions of the Iktomi and Miashla stories and I'd put several of them together to understand how to be more responsible for my actions and myself.

Remembering all of these things, not just the stories of Iktomi and Miashla, has steered me into the recognition of what it is to be Lakota, a human being. In doing so, I have found no place for the words, "good" or "bad," "right" or "wrong." Through this process and with help from nature's grandfathers, the rocks, the trees, the wind, I am beginning to see and to understand situations and people just as they are. I've had to teach myself to decide whether something or someone is healthy or unhealthy for me and not to judge what they are for others. I've come to realize that to judge a person from the position of being right or wrong prevented me from looking at them, or even myself, clearly and that in reality, prejudging was causing me to withdraw from the brotherhood of life to which the Lakota have always belonged.

For more than fifty years, I have tried to understand what this life is about. My thinking has been in fragments and disorganized until I began to remember and to put the pieces together. Now I see more clearly how my ancestors held onto their identity and to their relationship within the brotherhood of life. To know who you are and to face your fears and conquer them frees you to become a strong, contributing individual. I have come to understand more clearly the wisdom and knowledge that guided my ancestors for generations was designed to strengthen each individual, for that in turn strengthens the group and whatever weakens the individual weakens the group. I've learned that fear, anger, and the use of alcohol and other mind-altering drugs will fragment a person's mind and prevent him from hearing and seeing in a human way. It will stop him dead in his tracks from growing and keep him from truly becoming a compassionate, caring human being, a Lakota.

Now the fear created by those beatings is gone. The anger fueled by alcohol is gone. My mind is clear. Even today, after so many years, the memory of the elders who raised me is strong. I see now that throughout the most difficult times they walked straight-backed with clear and focused eyes that pierced through any pretense another person might have. They had no need to beat their children, their wives or each other. They had no need to shout out in angry voices. They kept their homes neat and the ground they lived on was clean and free of litter. They were Lakota and they knew it deep into their souls, each one expressing it in his individual style.

As Jane and I set these final words down on paper, my brother Ben passed away. The grief I feel washes over me in overwhelming waves. We Lakota call the acting out of grief, "cante sica," in English "heart bad." It can be different for each individual. Yet, as I mourn, my eyes are open to the beauty that surrounds me, the beauty of the earth, and the beauty of our people.

Within minutes of Ben's death, the phone started ringing: Friends and relatives from all over the country had begun reaching out. Some would question how the news could spread so fast. We call it "The Moccasin Telegraph." It just happens, no newspaper, radio station or TV broadcast—just caring people sharing with each other.

The burial process here on the reservation can take days of preparation. It was no different for Ben's funeral. Over the course of a week, there were many aspects to consider: Who will help to dig the grave? Are there enough shovels? Who has large pots? Where's the grate to put over the cooking fire? Not the least of our concerns was to watch the weather for the funeral procession would travel from the Catholic church at the massacre site over three miles of dirt road and field to our family's cemetery here at Mouse Creek. Any rain would cause that path to turn into thick, slippery mud. We never worry about how many will attend and how we will feed them, for, in our way, even complete strangers step forward to help and that's how it was for Ben.

His son in Colorado sent new clothes for Ben to wear, a white shirt, black vest, pants, and a western-style, black string tie. His oldest daughter stepped forward to lead us in organizing the burial arrangements. Soon a nearby rancher came offering two young heifers to be butchered for meat to feed our family and friends.

The following day, a neighbor arrived to butcher the heifers and, before we knew it, twelve people came to help. The rancher drove up with the cattle in his trailer and shot the animals. Their bodies were placed on the ground. Knives were sharpened and the group took turns, three or four at a time, skinning, quartering, and cutting the meat into steaks, which were placed in boxes lined with trash bags to be washed and distributed to cooks. They joked with each other as they worked, and my dog stood quietly by, wagging her tail in anticipation of handouts. The night before had brought on a frost, but the sun came out, pleasantly warming the day, and meadowlarks filled the air with their songs.

Two men brought over a backhoe to dig the grave. I was so relieved to have that burden lifted, for in the past we've often had to do the digging with hand shovels. Nephews brought a rough box on their pick-up truck to line the grave. The undertaker lent shovels for filling Ben's grave and thick straps to lower his coffin down.

We went into Gordon, Nebraska to shop for supplies and were greeted in the grocery store by an old friend of Ben's, a trapper named Decker, whom Ben had called J.D. He retold the story of how he came to be known simply as J.D. When they met, Ben had asked his name and he replied, "Decker." "Just Decker?" asked Ben. "Yes, just Decker." "Well," said Ben, "I'm going to call you J.D. then. Short for Just Decker." The trapper replied, "Then I'll call you, J.B. short for Just Ben." J.D. contributed two cans of coffee and a large sheet cake decorated with colorful horses.

Wherever we went, people came up to us offering condolences and their memories of different jokes Ben had told. Ben had lifted spirits and healed many people from sorrow and frustration through his down-to-earth humor.

We held a wake for two days and two nights in the church, before the funeral. As is our way, people of all ages stayed around the clock watching over Ben's body. As the hours passed, more and more people wandered in and out to pay their respects to Ben. Some sat off to the side lost in quiet thought, others gathered in groups, talking. Children played together, mothers soothed tired infants in their arms. Stories of Ben's teasing and joking were shared. Laughter filled the room.

Young adults in the family took turns cooking large pots of soup. Others carried in boxes of fry bread they had made at home, potato salad, bologna sandwiches, and beans. Hot coffee was always available, as well as jugs of juice and lemonade. Though it was the end of the month and funds for all reservation families were low, the food kept multiplying—like the loaves and fishes story in the Christian Bible story.

We placed large folding tables on either side of the coffin and covered them in bright-colored cloth. Ben's children put out pictures taken of Ben at various times in his life. In among the pictures, people placed flowers, cards, candles, and fancy cakes that have become popular to give.

Singers with guitars came in the evenings and filled the building with the melodies of old time western songs, hymns and traditional Lakota spiritual songs of prayer. Members from two American Legion groups on the reservation brought in flags to honor Ben, who had been a veteran during the Korean War.

A spring snow started falling on the second day of the wake. It covered everything in a thick wet blanket, inches deep. The storm lasted well into the night and by morning, the long road to the family cemetery had turned slick with mud. Young men came to clear the grave of snow and the funeral plans were revised to fit the conditions. At last, we gathered again in the church. A priest friend led us in the final prayers for Ben and the crowd stood and followed as his coffin was carried outside to a waiting pickup truck. The men from the American Legion gathered one last time. They took a final roll call, calling out his name three times, fired off a twenty-one-gun salute and filled the silence with the sound of a bugle playing "Taps."

A few of us with four-wheel-drive vehicles proceeded over the treacherous, slippery dirt road to the family cemetery. As some got bogged down and stuck in the mud, we moved the coffin from one truck to another. We were certain Ben found something humorous in that. Finally, we were there.

Metal pipes had been laid across the top of the grave to help the pallbearers roll the coffin in place. They placed movers straps around it, pulled the pipes out of the way, and lowered the coffin down; with the rough box cover lowered on top of it. One young man jumped down to nail the box shut. Once he climbed back out, we prayed one last time and then watched as people took turns shoveling in the dirt.

The group returned to the church where the rest had waited to share one last meal. A fire had been built outside earlier in the day to cook large pots of soup. Folding tables had been set up in the church basement; the food was placed on them along with the paper plates and plastic utensils. Once everyone had had their fill, Ben's children began the "giveaway." People sat in folding chairs around the perimeter of the room as various items, blankets, socks, towels, were given to the guests and family members. One by one, they filed out and the church was empty. The week was over. Ben was going home. I will not say his name again until I know he's safely there.

Today, I stand facing the sunset where my Lakota grandparents have gone home. I acknowledge their wisdom, courage, and generosity. I am grateful to them. Through their efforts, I have dignity, respect, honor, and pride. I can face the future until I go home to join them.

The tree, the wind, the rocks, the sky and others are also my grandparents. They continue to give me strength and direction. They have endured throughout my life and will remain long after I am gone. Because I have remembered the lessons from my Lakota elders and nature's elders, I am discovering who I am, and the dark fog has lifted. I can finally hear the Creator, touch the Creator, taste the Creator, smell the Creator, and see the Creator. I am able to say, "I am a Lakota. I am a human being. I belong to the brotherhood of life."

CPSIA information can be obtained
at www.ICGtesting.com
Printed in the USA
LVHW051651180123
737311LV00004B/345